Food Processor
Cookery

Food Processor Cookery

by Michael Barry

ictc

First published 1983 by the Publishing Division of ICTC Ltd.,
632-652 London Road, Isleworth, Middlesex, TW13 4EZ

British Library Cataloguing in Publication Data

Barry, Michael
    Michael Barry's food processor cookery
    1. Food processor cookery
    I. Title
    641.5'89   TX840.F6

ISBN 0 907642 09 8
ISBN 0 907642 08 X Pbk

Design and photography by Edward Piper
Edited by Tessa Hayward

Food for photographs by Joanna Benson

Printed in Great Britain by Chorley & Pickersgill Ltd, Leeds

ICTC Stock Number: 54128

The author and publisher would like to thank Divertimenti,
68-72 Marylebone Lane, London W1M 5FF for the loan of the
accessories used in the photographs on pages 15, 65

The dishes and china on pages 19, 25, 28, 34, 43, 57, 91, 99, 119
are from ICTC Ltd.

contents

Chapter		Page
	Introduction	10
1	Dip in	13
2	Country kitchen soups	18
3	Perfect pâtés and potted meats	29
4	Dressy dressings and super sauces	36
5	Salads and crudites	44
6	Eggs are exciting	55
7	Something special — food for parties	63
8	Marvellous mince	73
9	And so to veg	78
10	Pastry makes perfect	90
11	Bread is beautiful	107
12	Crafty cakes	117
13	Proven puddings	126
14	Shake it honey	134

Welcome to the Processor Revolution: One of the great changes in your life. If you think that's a bit exaggerated, I promise you it's not. A processor really does make a fundamental difference, not only to how hard you have to work, but also to the kind of dishes that you can manage. There are a whole lot of things that now take me a matter of moments and that I wouldn't have dreamed of trying a couple of years ago.

Pâtés and pastry, sauces and soups, dips and delicious desserts. Dishes a professional chef would think highly skilled and time consuming are made not only simple but almost shamefully quickly. That's why ALL the top French restaurants use food processors as a matter of course and why the revolution is now taking place in your home too.

A processor isn't just for special cooking and grand occasions alone. If it was it would still be worth it, but for me the reason why a processor has pride of place in my kitchen before every other tool, except my knives, is that I use it all the time to do every day tasks . . . chopping a handful of parsley, slicing a cucumber, making salad dressing. Things I can and have done by hand, but a processor just does it better, quicker and easier. And that's the true secret, I don't use it as a gadget to be got out at odd intervals, I use it all the time, casually and without thinking about it. There are, of course, things a processor won't do; mash potatoes (they wind up like glue), or whip egg whites (without a special attachment). And there are things that it will do that are simply quicker or easier by hand. For example I always beat the eggs for an omelette by hand. But for making bread crumbs, blending a white sauce, chopping onions, creating an instant soup from left overs, I just wouldn't be without it.

There is one more important bonus for you, and your family, and that is quality. If you have ever made bread, and wished it had a smoother texture, wait until you knead the next batch in your processor. The smoothest, best risen crumb ever. Or do you have mayonnaise with a mind of its own? Separating and curdling? Just try the recipe on page 39 and you will never keep a standby jar again.

This book's hope is to make cooking more fun and eating more exciting. There are both every-day recipes and grand ones. Cooking with a processor is so quick that sometimes I have given more than one recipe for similar sorts of dishes, try both and see which you like best. Please use your own favourite recipes too! This is not a comprehensive list of all that a processor can do, it's a collection of my favourites, and I hope an introduction to some of the unexpected and delicious sides of life that are now yours to look (and cook) forward to with your processor.

Making friends with your processor

Do make friends with your processor, get to know it . . . take it apart and put it together until you can do it without worrying. Let me introduce you properly.

Every processor, whatever the make, has three basic sections. Firstly there is the motor section. Food processors come with two different kinds of motor. The best, the strongest and the quietest is the direct drive motor. This is a very heavy and reliable motor with only one moving part. It has a constant speed, and takes up power as it is needed, so that a few sprigs of parsley or a full load of meat are chopped at the same speed.

The other kind usually has a faster running motor which is belt driven or geared, and therefore adjusts its speed to the load in it and is inclined to slow down quite a lot with a thick heavy mixture. With some models this slowing down is partly overcome by switches to vary the speed of the motor, however, these machines have the disadvantage that the belts wear out and then break.

Some processors have a cut out switch to prevent overloading. The instructions will have a method to be followed if this happens, it varies from machine to machine.

The next section is the bowl. This will have three

The crafty cook adding soy sauce to mixed fried vegetables
(see page 82)

parts . . . the bowl itself, the lid, and a pusher of some kind to put foods through the slicing or grating discs. Practice putting on the bowl and the lid a few times until you are familiar with the system.

The third section is the tools. There are three tools standard to all processors and almost countless accessories to fit individual models. The standard ones are; **the Double-Bladed Knife**. This is the key tool in any processor, the workhorse of the system. It will chop, blend, purée, liquidise, mix, mince, knead bread and make pastry and it will probably do more things that I haven't thought of yet. It shouldn't need sharpening or adjusting for many years. Some processors also have a plastic blade that looks similar, and they recommend for beating and

mixing batters etc. and some come with a plastic dough blade, which has been specially shaped to evenly knead the maximum quantity of bread. **The Grater**. This tool does all the work of an ordinary grater with two real advantages, you never get your finger nails grated (or even your fingers) and the blade really does work, at a phenomenal speed. Some models have various sized graters for different sized results. **The Slicing Disc**. Once again these come in a variety of thicknesses and for some machines a selection is available including ripple edges, etc. I find the thinest slicing disc the most useful, except for potatoes which need at least a 1/4 in. for anything except crisps. Make sure you keep control of the way you feed food into the slicer as this can make a lot of difference to the evenness and the neatness of the result.

Variations. There are specialist discs and blades available for some machines, and one machine in particular that has the complete range. These accessories are too many and various to list, but they do all add to the versatility of your processor and are well worth collecting.

A couple of discs that most people have and found useful and interesting are:

The Chipping Disc. This not only cuts chips effortlessly and beautifully finely, it also can cut other vegetables into strips for casseroles or chinese style stir frying. **The Coleslaw or Julienne Cutter**. This is the very coarse style grater that I use to make delicate strip garnishes for soups or, to provide salad or 'crudite' vegetables with a slight crunch to them.

Whatever tools you have in the original pack, take time to get to know them. A food processor itself is NOT a gadget; it is an everyday tool, a constant helper in the kitchen. Wait until you have a really busy days cooking to do and then use your processor for everything you conceivably can. You will swiftly learn, the many and sometimes unexpected ways it will make cooking easier, quicker and not least more fun. Practice with it, on cheap or bulk ingredients, until you feel really at home and you will truly have become part of the Processor Revolution.

Guacamole, crab dip, blue cheese and apple dip arranged with a selection of vegetables and home fried crisps

dip in

Dips are really an American habit which has happily caught on on this side of the Atlantic. A variety of creamy smooth pâté type dishes, they are nicest eaten by dipping something crisp into them and putting it straight in your mouth. They are perfect with drinks before dinner, or, on a larger scale, as something to serve at a party without having to get into a full scale buffet. They also make something rather nice to nibble while watching the telly, or listening to your favourite record, whether it's Beethoven, Bream or the Beatles.

The best way to serve dips is in small and attractive pottery dishes with straight sides, about 1½ in. deep. The little French soufflé dishes are ideal for this, as are many of the products now being turned out by the handicraft potteries that seem to have sprung up by the hundred throughout Britain in the last couple of years.

To serve with them, the classic dipping tool is the crisp. However if you're a bit of a purist, why not try making your own. After all, with a processor the hard work is done for you. Just peel 2 or 3 potatoes, trim them to fit in the feed-tube, slice them, wash the slices in a little running water (you don't have to take them out of the bowl to do that); drain them and then deep fry them, a handful at a time, in hot oil just below smoking temperature – 30 seconds is enough – followed by a minute or two out of the fat, and then fry for another 45 seconds. (Don't forget to salt them before you let them cool for the second time. And if you have to store them for long make sure it's in an air-tight tin.)

If you don't fancy crisps, or there are weight-watchers about, try serving your dips with carrots, thinly sliced lengthwise, (you can use the processor) or chunks of celery. I've even had success with tiny raw cauliflower florets; try it, they're amazingly crunchy and taste delicious, especially with the cheesy dips.

As for the dips themselves, because a processor makes them all in a matter of seconds, you can make two or three with contrasting flavours and textures. For a really show-off spread my favourites include Guacamole, Crab, and Blue Cheese and Apple. But any of them is delicious on its own. One word of warning. If you're planning to serve a meal afterwards don't serve too many or too big portions of dips. They are surprisingly tempting.

yoghurt and mint

This dip is to be found under a variety of names all over the Middle East from Persia right across to Morocco. Its popularity is based both on the marriage of the flavours and on the cooling effect that the mint has both on spicy food and on fiery climates. It's a summer dip, and one to remind you of an exotic holiday, or maybe just a romantic dream under the desert sky.

Double-bladed knife
¾ pint (450 ml) plain natural yoghurt (as thick as possible)
1 teaspoon salt
1 tablespoon lemon juice
6 sprigs fresh washed mint

Put the yoghurt, lemon juice and salt into the bowl. Cover and process for 5 seconds until blended. Strip the mint leaves (it has to be fresh mint, dried mint just doesn't work properly with this dish) from the stalks, switch the motor on and add the leaves in two or three lots so that the first lot is completely blended into the yoghurt and the last lot still retains some semblance of separate identity. The process should take about 10 to 15 seconds. Pour into shallow bowls. In the Middle East this is often eaten using the inner leaves of a cos lettuce as spoons, an interesting and original alternative to our idea of pouring the dressing over the salad.

Putting yoghurt, lemon juice and salt into the bowl

Adding the mint while processing

Pouring the dip into serving ramekins

guacamole

Guacamole is perhaps the most famous of all the avocado dishes that come from Mexico, which is where the avocado was first really developed. In its homeland Guacamole is a smooth creamy compliment to the very spicy dishes that so often appear on the Mexican table; the recipe below doesn't include any chili, although if you fancy yourself as a real *compañero* you can always add a pinch. If you're feeling really *olé* try your Guacamole with the Chili con Carne recipe on page 77 for a really terrific *Tijuana* tea time.

Double-bladed knife
1 medium green pepper
1 small onion
3 medium tomatoes
1 large ripe avocado
2 tablespoons salad oil
1 tablespoon lemon or fresh lime juice
salt and pepper

Cut the green pepper in half and take out all the seeds. Cut each half in four and place in the bowl together with the peeled and quartered onion, and the quartered tomatoes. Process for 5 seconds or until the vegetables are still in pieces but well cut up and mixed. Cut the avocado in half, remove the stone and keep it. Scoop out the flesh which should be soft, but not discoloured. Place it in the bowl. Add the oil and lemon or lime juice, half a teaspoon of salt, a sprinkling of black pepper and, if you fancy it, a pinch of chili. Process for 10 seconds. Stop to scrape down the sides, before processing for another 2 seconds, then pile it into a serving bowl. If you are going to store the Guacamole for more than half an hour before serving it, place the stone in the centre of the full bowl, and cover with cling film. There is a chemical in the stone that stops the avocado flesh from turning brown.

Variation: **Tomato Guacamole**

If you would like to serve the Guacamole as an interesting and unusual starter reduce the number of tomatoes to one, make it as before, but to serve it, take a large ripe tomato for each person. Cut a lid off the top about a quarter of the way down, scoop out the flesh with a teaspoon (saving it for the Tomato and Orange Soup on page 21), sprinkle a little salt into the tomato cases and fill with the Guacamole mixture.
Put the lids back on at a jaunty angle and chill in the refrigerator for 45 minutes before serving.

Olé – chili con carne, mixed rice and sweetcorn, guacamole

blue cheese and apple

Cheese and apple is a favourite combination for puddings in many parts of the world. This dip combines the two and has the added attraction of a really unusual texture coming from the grated apple, whose sweetness counteracts the bite of the cheese. It's a strong, definite flavour, and one to serve on its own if you're looking for a single dip, but is equally good in the company of others.

Grating disc
Double-bladed knife
2 eating apples
6 oz (175 g) Danish Blue cheese
1/2 cup milk
1 desertspoon lemon juice
salt and pepper

Core but don't peel the apples. Cut them into quarters and grate them into the bowl. Tip them out, and add the lemon juice to prevent discolouration. Fit the double-bladed knife and into the bowl (which doesn't need washing), put the broken up blue cheese, cover and switch on. Add the milk in a slow steady stream until the mixture blends smoothly. Put the apple back in, season, and process again for not more than 2 or 3 seconds just to blend together.

sour cream and onion

People have been known to make this dip using a packet of onion soup. Indeed, when caught short, and before food processors arrived, I have done it myself. But with a processor there are no excuses; and it's just as quick to do it the right way.

Double-bladed knife
1 bunch spring onions
2 chicken stock cubes
2 cartons sour cream
salt

Clean the spring onions, keeping the green as well as the white parts. Cut them into 1 in. lengths; put them in the bowl. Add the chicken stock cubes, and process until they're finely chopped (7 seconds). Scrape the sides down,

add the sour cream and process again until the whole mixture is amalgamated. Taste, you may want to add a little more salt. When it's seasoned, pour it into its serving dish. A little of the chopped spring onions, saved before adding the sour cream, sprinkled over the top, makes a nice garnish to this lovely pale green piquant dish.

egg and tomato

This dip's a bit of a cheat really, because it's a version of one of my favourite sandwich fillings. In fact, if you have any left over, unlikely though that turns out to be in my experience, it does make a lovely sandwich the next day. Very cheap to make, and one of the dips that's especially popular with children, if you've got a birthday party or a picnic coming up.

Double-bladed knife
3 tomatoes
3 eggs
1 tablespoon butter
2 tablespoons mayonnaise (see page 39)
salt and pepper

Cut the peeled tomatoes into quarters, and process for 3 or 4 seconds until roughly chopped. Scramble the eggs with butter until set but not rubbery. Off the heat, stir in the mayonnaise. Allow to cool a moment, and then add to the bowl and process for 5 seconds more to thoroughly mix the tomatoes and egg. This looks particularly pretty piled into white china dishes. It can be served with fingers of toast as an alternative to the more orthodox dipping tools.

cheese and date

This unlikely combination was taught to me by a lady who was deeply concerned with health foods and wholemeal eating. She believed it contained some of the basic ingredients for good health. I think she may be right. It also contains some splendid flavours for those of us less rigorous about our diets. It's a dip that really doesn't go well with crisps and the ideal dipping sticks, I think, are chunks of fresh, crisp celery.

Double-bladed knife
3 oz (75 g) stoneless dates
8 oz (225 g) cream cheese
2 teaspoons lemon juice
4 tablespoons milk
salt

Put the dates in the bowl and process until fairly finely chopped (about 5 seconds). Scrape down the sides if necessary. Add the cream cheese, the milk, the lemon juice and a good pinch of salt. Process again for 10 seconds, until the dates and cheese are well blended. Be careful not to process for too long, it's really at its best when the dates still have a certain texture and bite left to them.

crab dip

This is an adaptation of a famous Cornish treat; a part of the world where the fisherman's catch and the farmer's produce get blended together to make some of the most delicious food in the British Isles. It's ideal if you can get fresh, or even frozen crab meat, but even if you can't, a tin of crab meat out of the larder makes a delicious dip. In the South West of England they use clotted cream in this recipe, so if you can find it, do use it. For the rest of us ordinary human beings, cottage cheese makes an adequate substitute.

Double-bladed knife
6 oz (175 g) cottage cheese
2 spring onions
4 tablespoons top of the milk
1 teaspoon made English mustard
6 oz (175 g) crab meat
salt and pepper

Put the cottage cheese and the milk in the bowl and process until really smooth (about 15 seconds). Scrape down the sides and add the mustard, the cleaned spring onions cut into 1 in. lengths and a little salt and pepper. Process again (5 seconds) until the onion is chopped up but has not vanished. Add the crab meat, making sure to have taken out any bits of shell. Process for another 5 seconds. Pile into a serving dish and rough up the surface with a fork. It will set quite firm if left in the fridge for an hour or more.

country kitchen soups

One of the biggest surprises that a processor brings to the kitchen is home-made soups. Now that soup has for so long come out of a tin or a packet, most of us have forgotten how cheap it is to make at home, how delicious it tastes and, now how easy and quick it can be too. There are a whole range of soups here, going from the meal-in-a-bowl of Chunky Chicken, through the famous French Onion, covered in crisp toasted bread and bubbling cheese, – to the delicate cold haute cuisine flavour of Vichyssoise, swirling with cream, or the exotic Spanish soup, Gazpacho. What they all share is a freshness and an extraordinary strength of flavour. I think the reputation that country kitchens have for home-cooked food with really heartening flavours, derives from their soups.

A little word about stock before we begin the soups themselves. In all these recipes where stock is recommended, you can use the ready-made cubed chicken or beef stocks, but *do* try making your own stock. I'm sure many of these soups are going to become family favourites, and delicious though they are, they are even more special if you make them with the almost free ingredients that home-made stock needs. For example a chicken carcase, either raw (after the portions have been cut off it to cook separately), or the left-over bones from a roast chicken (on condition it hasn't been stuffed) simmered with a bay leaf and an onion for an hour, makes a couple of pints of stock of such good flavour that you could amost drink it on its own. Most butchers will give you a couple of beef bones, cut up, which will make beef stock with two hours of gentle simmering (less with a pressure cooker). It will have the kind of deep flavour that no packet can ever produce. Either way, I think that you're going to find that the new help in the kitchen makes a difference to your starters, especially when eaten with one of the home-baked breads you can find on pages 106-115.

Spinach soup

spinach soup

This is a soup you can make without stock, and using frozen spinach. Whether you make it with fresh or frozen spinach, the butter is quite important, even though the quantity may seem generous. Spinach and butter go especially well together, and they combine to make a soup of delicate flavour and extremely beautiful colour. Even those in your family who don't much fancy looking like Popeye are going to enjoy this one.

Double-bladed knife
1½ lb (675 g) fresh or ½ lb (225 g) cooked, frozen spinach
3 oz (75 g) butter
½ pint (300 ml) water
¾ pint (450 ml) milk
1 teaspoon cornflour
salt and pepper

If you're using fresh spinach, wash it carefully and rough-chop it with a knife so that it's in inch wide ribbons, having discarded any tough stalks. From there on you proceed the same way whether it's fresh or frozen. Melt 2 oz (50 g) of the butter in a deep saucepan, and add the spinach. Stir to coat well with the butter. Add the water, cover the pan and simmer until the spinach is well cooked but not khaki coloured. Four to five minutes for fresh, and until it's just melted for frozen spinach, is the right length of time. Pour the spinach mixture into the processor, process for 20 seconds or until the spinach is very finely chopped indeed. You may need to stop and scrape the sides down once or twice during this process. Return the spinach purée to the pan, add the milk, having saved a little bit to mix the cornflour into a smooth paste. Add the cornflour paste, and, stirring thoroughly, bring the whole soup up gently to the boil. When it's thickened, season it well and serve it with a tiny nob of butter for each bowl. It should be pale green, flecked with little specks of darker green from the spinach leaves.

potage bonne femme

The Good Womans Soup – unfussy, and yet perfectly balanced, easy to do and difficult to get perfect – that is, until the food processor came along. There are a number of slight variants on this soup and my favourite version has a delicate variety of colours and a subtle blend of flavours. It's quite important not to over process this soup as it's not meant to be completely smooth, but to have a little texture left in the vegetables.

Double-bladed knife
¾ lb (350 g) potatoes
½ lb (225 g) carrots
½ lb (225 g) leeks
2 oz (50 g) butter
bunch of parsley
1 pint (600 ml) stock
½ pint (300 ml) milk
salt and pepper

Cut all the peeled vegetables into 1 in. chunks and fry them gently in the butter in a deep saucepan until they are thoroughly coated. Add the stock, but not the milk; season and simmer for 20 minutes. Meanwhile process the washed and dried parsley until finely chopped. Take out and reserve. Put the vegetables and stock into the bowl. (Unless you have one of the very big machines you will probably have to process the soup in two batches.) Switch on and process for 10 seconds, then check to see there are no big lumps of vegetables, but rather, a fine mince. Return to the saucepan, add the milk, and a little more water if the soup is of too thick a consistency. Heat through and serve in individual bowls, sprinkled thickly with the chopped parsley. Once again, crusty French bread is the ideal accompaniment.

tomato and orange

This is really one of the craftiest soups of all, as the ingredients can be kept in the larder until they are needed, but that doesn't stop it being very delicious and unusual. Don't tell your guests what's in it until after they have had a taste, for the proof of the soup, as well as the pudding, is in the eating.

Double-bladed knife
One 1 lb (450 g) tin Italian tomatoes (or 1 lb (450 g) fresh)
1 medium sized onion
2 oz (50 g) butter
1 pint (600 ml) orange juice (carton is best)
generous pinch sugar
salt and pepper

Chop the onion; fry it in the butter until soft but not brown. Add the tomatoes and orange juice. Simmer together for 15 minutes until the tomatoes are thoroughly cooked. Process until completely smooth, adding the pinch of sugar while the blades are working. Taste for seasoning – it will need a good large pinch of salt – and serve it, hot with a few thinly cut orange slices floating on the top.

carrot soup

The lovely golden colour of this soup makes it extremely appetising, especially on a cold winter's day. The yoghurt is not traditional, but rather a modern, crafty touch – try it anyway, it cuts the sweetness of the carrots just perfectly for my taste.

Double-bladed knife
1½ lb (675 g) carrots
2 medium sized potatoes
2 onions
1½ pints (900 ml) chicken stock
½ teaspoon turmeric
1 carton natural yoghurt
1-2 tablespoons oil

Peel the vegetables and cut them into chunks. Toss all the vegetables in a deep saucepan with a little oil to prevent them sticking, and sprinkle over the turmeric. Turn them until thoroughly coated. Add the chicken stock then bring to the boil and simmer on a medium heat for 25 minutes with a lid on the saucepan. Take out all the vegetables and enough stock to make a purée. Place in the bowl and process for 15 seconds. Return to the saucepan, season, heat through and pour into a tureen. Beat the pot of yoghurt until it's smooth and slightly runny, and stir it into the soup so that it swirls into a marble pattern.

In Eastern Europe they sometimes make a soup similar to this with a few caraway seeds added at the frying stage at the beginning. They make an interesting and unusual flavour alternative.

lentil soup

Rich warming lentil soups always seem to be a thing of legend or family reminiscence, but in fact they are one of the easiest in the world to make. And there *is* nothing more comforting and warming in the middle of a chill winter than a bowl of steaming lentil soup, – fragrant with herbs, and really quite effortless to prepare.

Double-bladed knife
3/4 lb (350 g) red or green lentils
processor chopped parsley and chives
2 pints (1200 ml) beef stock (water will do, but is not so nice)
2 onions
2 carrots
1 teaspoon black treacle
1½ oz (30 g) butter
salt and pepper

Fry the lentils, (which you have carefully made sure contain no small stones) in the butter, with the onions and carrots both peeled and cut into chunks. Turn until thoroughly coated with the butter then add the stock and simmer for 25 minutes for red lentils, or 35 for green. If all the liquid is being used up, add another half a pint of water. Pour half the mixture into the processor including all the large chunks of vegetables. Process until smooth; return to the pan; stir thoroughly and reheat. Serve with a little nob of butter and a sprinkling of parsley and chives in each bowl.

fancy fish soup

This recipe has both Scottish and Mediterranean ancestors. What they both share, is a real liking for rich flavoured soups made with the produce of the sea. The recipe for this is extremely economical, as any good fishmonger should let you have (when you're buying something else, of course) a couple of good fish heads, preferably cod, halibut or turbot. You can use specially bought fish, but there's actually more flavour in the head. Don't let the eyes put you off.

Double-bladed knife
A couple of large fish heads or 1½ lb (675 g) assorted fish
     trimmings
1 clove garlic
1 large onion
1 small 7 oz (175 g) tin tomatoes
bay leaf
bunch of parsley
3 tablespoons lemon juice
salt and pepper

Wash the fish heads (or fish), place in a large saucepan and cover generously with water – the amount depends on the size of the heads and the saucepan. Bring to the boil, skimming off any froth that rises. Add the bay leaf, parsley and the lemon juice, cover and simmer for 40 minutes. Remove the fish heads from the stock, to which you add the clove of garlic, peeled and cut into quarters; the onion likewise, and the tin of tomatoes. Simmer the stock for another 15 minutes with the vegetables in it. Process for 20 seconds, until thoroughly blended, and then add half the flesh from the fish heads or the fish (there's a surprising amount on fish heads – don't be put off by the look of them), and process until smooth. Pour the mixture back into the pan, cook for a further 10 minutes. Season highly, and serve over the remaining fish in chunks. This dish really needs lots of good, fresh bread and butter and can make a generous meal in its own right.

Fish head and bones placed in a large saucepan

Preparing the garlic and lemon

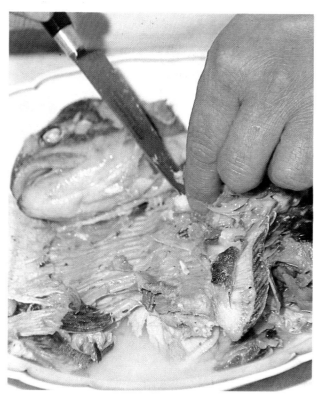

Boning the cooked fish

Adding some of the fish stock to the processor bowl

Returning the mixture to the remaining stock in the bowl

chunky chicken chowder

This is the ideal dish to make if you have the remains of a carcase of a chicken. It's another 'meal in a bowl', similar in some ways to the American chowders that have become almost legendary because of their savoury richness.

Double-bladed knife
1 raw chicken carcase
2 pints (1200 ml) water
bay leaf
celery stalk
head of parsley
1 large onion
small packet mixed, frozen vegetables
1 egg
1 teaspoon cornflour
salt and pepper

Cover the carcase with water, bring to the boil, skim off any froth. Add the herbs and celery; cover and simmer for 1 hour. Remove the bones and chicken meat from the liquid and pour the stock into the bowl. Switch on, add the cornflour mixed with a little cold water and the egg. Process until smooth, return to the pan; cook over a gentle heat until the mixture thickens, just below the boil. Add the onion, chopped finely (you can do this in the processor bowl without washing it out again) and the packet of frozen mixed vegetables which do not need to be defrosted or cooked. Simmer for just 5 minutes. Remove any good meat from the chicken carcass. Cut it into chunks; add it to the soup; and serve, well seasoned, in a large tureen.

french onion soup

This recipe is always preceded in cookery books with tales of how the writer first had it early one morning in Les Halles, the famous fruit and vegetable market in Paris. Unfortunately, by the time I got there they were pulling Les Halles down, but I've managed to eat it in a number of French restaurants both in France and throughout the world, and I can verify the genuine Gallic taste in this version. And you don't have to be up at 6 a.m. to taste it!

Slicing disc
Grating disc
2 lb (900 g) onions
1 oz (25 g) beef dripping
1 teaspoon sugar
2 pints (1200 ml) beef stock
1 desertspoon Worcester sauce
1/2 French loaf
4 oz (100 g) cheese (Gruyère is perfect, Gouda is fine)
salt and pepper

Peel and halve the onions and put them through the slicing disc. Melt the dripping and fry the onions mixed with the teaspoon of sugar until they are brown but not burnt. This should take about 5 minutes over a medium heat. The sugar will help to caramelise them and produce the rich dark flavour and colour characteristic of this soup. Add the Worcester sauce and a seasoning of salt and pepper; pour over the stock and simmer very gently for at least 35 minutes, stirring occasionally. The onions should almost melt into the soup, but still have a slight texture of their own. Cut the French bread into 1/4 in. slices and put these to toast in a low oven, while you grate, into a clean, dry bowl, the cheese. To serve the soup, put a ladleful into each fire-proof dish, float a piece of the toast on the top, and heap some grated cheese on top of that. Cook under the grill for just a minute until the cheese is melted, and serve bubbling hot, being careful not to eat it too quickly lest you singe your tongue, in the enthusiasm.

A sizzling bowl of french onion soup

vichyssoise

This is a cold soup, made of very ordinary ingredients like leeks and potatoes, but when properly blended and served with a swirl of ice cold cream it is one of the great haute cuisine dishes of restaurants around the world. It's supposed to have been developed in America, when a French chef, who'd made it as a hot soup was kept waiting so long by an insensitive guest he let the soup get cold and added the cream as a last minute guilty thought. Whether that story is true or not, it's certainly worth your while trying it without any guilt whatsoever.

Double-bladed knife
1½ lb (675 g) potatoes
1½ lb (675 g) leeks
1 onion
2 tablespoons oil
1½ pints (900 ml) chicken stock
4 oz (100 g) double cream
salt and pepper

Peel the potatoes and onion and cut into 1 in. sized cubes. Peel the broken leaves off the leeks. Slice them in half lengthwise and leave in cold water for at least 10 minutes before washing thoroughly to clear all the dirt out. Cut into 1 in. lengths and fry gently, with the onion and potatoes, in oil for 5 minutes or until all the vegetables are softened. Add a good pinch of salt and pepper, cover with the stock and simmer for 30 minutes. The vegetables should be completely soft but not disintegrated. Add all the vegetables and enough stock to let the blades work, to the bowl. Process until the vegetables are completely smooth, adding a little more stock if necessary as they blend. Return the mixture to the remaining stock in the saucepan and stir until completely smooth. Pour into a bowl and chill in the refrigerator for at least 2 hours until thoroughly cold. To serve, ladle the soup into individual bowls, swirl the double cream around the top so it forms a spiral, and sprinkle the top of the soup with some freshly chopped green chives. If there aren't any available use the freeze-dried version instead. Serve it with hot French bread, lashings of butter and bags of confidence.

gazpacho

This is an unusual soup from the Andalusian region of Spain. There are a number of different versions of it, ranging from a thin, garlicky liquid with a few bits and pieces floating around in it, to a full scale salad which couldn't be called a soup with the best will in the world. This is one of my favourites to serve on a hot summer's day, especially at a weekend buffet party. If you are a bit nervous about the garlic, you can cut down on it, but try not to leave it out altogether. My version falls somewhere between the extremes of the do-it-yourself-dinner-party Gazpacho and the thin-as-dish-water Gazpacho, both of which have their supporters.

Grating disc
Double-bladed knife
1 cucumber
1 Spanish onion
½ lb (225 g) tomatoes
1 clove garlic
1 small green pepper
2 × 1 in. slices wholemeal bread
2 tablespoons each, lemon juice and olive oil
One 20 oz (600 ml) tin tomato juice
½ pint (300 ml) water
salt and pepper

Grate the unpeeled cucumber. Empty the bowl, (there is no need to wash it), put in the knife. Add the quartered onion and the garlic and process until finely chopped. Add the quartered tomatoes and cleaned green pepper and process again for 2 seconds. Add half the tomato juice, the oil and the lemon juice and process for 5 seconds. Pour into a bowl, stir in the remaining tomato juice, the water and the cucumber. Season quite strongly with salt and pepper, and a pinch of sugar if the soup lacks sweetness from the tomatoes. Cut the bread into 1 in. cubes and place in a bowl on the table. Chill the soup in the fridge for at least an hour, and before serving add a couple of ice cubes per person. To serve it, ladle it into bowls and add the brown bread cubes individually to people's choice. A little grated cucumber and chopped onion and tomato mixture, kept separately in small bowls, can be added at the table if you choose, and is really quite *'olé!'*

Gazpacho makes a lovely cool and summery starter

Duck pâté en croûte served with a garnish of orange slices and parsley

perfect pâtés and potted meats

Once upon a time, apart from the professionals, only a few brave and dedicated souls ever tried to make pâté at home, and those who did used to dedicate an evening or most of a weekend day to the exhausting process of cutting up, mincing, blending and then cleaning the equipment afterwards. The results were usually worth it – pâtés, that not only tasted a great deal better, but cost a great deal less than those in the shops. For that small and dedicated band, of whom I am one, the processor has changed our way of life. What used to take an hour and a half now takes five minutes, and amazingly, the result is, if anything, even better; because when processing meat for a pâté, none of the juices are squeezed out as in conventional mincing; but rather, the meat is sliced super fine. The old cookery books used to instruct chefs, who had plenty of junior skivvies and helpers, to finely chop the meat, with great semi-circular blades called 'hachoirs', now the *little* semi-circular blades on the processor will do the same job in a great deal less time.

There's a range of pâtés here, from the super simple of the humble mackerel, to probably the most grand pâté of all, Duck en Croûte. There are also a number of recipes for potted meats and fish. These are in fact the British equivalent of pâtés, developed over many centuries, reaching their high point in the Edwardian period when they so often formed the centre of the incredible, heavily laden breakfast tables of the time. As starters or picnic food, or even, sandwich fillers, they take a lot of beating. They have the advantage as well, which isn't true of pâtés, that they can be served in tiny individual sized pots so that each diner can have one himself.

The potting has another advantage, it is the perfect way of using up left-over pieces that normally have to be discarded just as scraps. For flavour also, I think in many ways our potted meats can match many of the Continent's pâtés. Either way, you're in for a real treat with a range that no delicatessen could think of matching.

duck pâté en croûte

Without fear of contradiction *the* most exotic and delicious pâté I know. The whole duck roast, spiced, spiked with orange, baked in a buttery pastry case produces the perfect centre piece for a grand buffet, or the first course for a really very, very special meal indeed. Now I must say that this recipe isn't cheap and it's usually not quick; while a processor doesn't make it any cheaper, it certainly does make it easier to do. Indeed, I don't think I'd be willing to try it these days without the benefit of my special friend in the kitchen.

This is a pâté to be eaten with a knife and fork, not bread and butter; and a mild mango chutney or some French grainy mustard go marvellously with it.

Double-bladed knife
1 whole duck
juice and grated rind of 2 oranges
1 large onion
2 cloves garlic
1/2 teaspoon ground allspice
salt and pepper

pastry:
1 egg
4 oz (100 g) butter
6 oz (150 g) flour

Wash the duck thoroughly in very hot water; pat dry inside and out and put to roast in a hot, mark 6, 400°F, 200°C, oven on a rack in a baking tray. Do not prick it, coat it or adjust it. Let it roast for 1 hour. In the meantime prepare the pastry in the same way as the shortcrust pastry on page 97. Take it out, and put it to cool in the fridge. When the duck has roasted, take it out and allow it to cool slightly. Take the meat off the bones, keeping aside one half of the breast. Process the quartered onion and the garlic until finely chopped, add the duck meat and skin (except for the reserved breast) and process until fairly fine, add 4 tablespoons of the drippings from the roasting pan, the spice, seasonings, orange juice and rind, and process again for 3 seconds. Take a full size loaf tin and place the pastry ball in the base of it. Using your knuckles spread it quickly up the sides of the tin and across the bottom so it forms a complete casing. It doesn't need to be totally level on the inside, but it does need to have no breaks. Half fill this casing with the duck mixture, then put thin slices of the reserved breast in lengthwise down the middle of the mixture before covering with the remaining duck mixture and a sheet of foil. Bake in the high oven, mark 6, 400°F, 200°C, for 40 minutes. Turn down the heat to mark 4, 350°F, 175°C and remove the foil. Bake for another 10–15 minutes. Allow to cool, and slipping a knife carefully around the edges of the loaf tin (non-stick tins really are the secret for this) ease the pâté out so that its crisp, golden exterior is uppermost. Leave it in a cool place – not the fridge (the pastry will go soggy) – overnight, and serve it cut, with a very sharp knife into 1 in. slices.

A slight variation is to add a couple of tablespoons of green peppercorns when you put the slices of duck breast into the middle of the pâté, they add a sharpness and an unusual texture to what is a very special dish indeed.

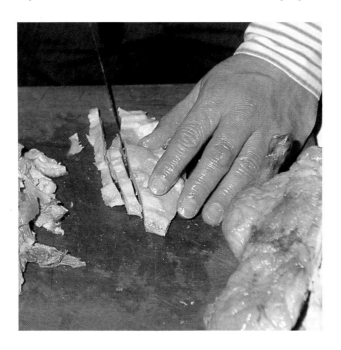

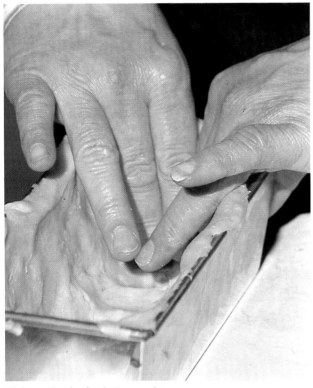

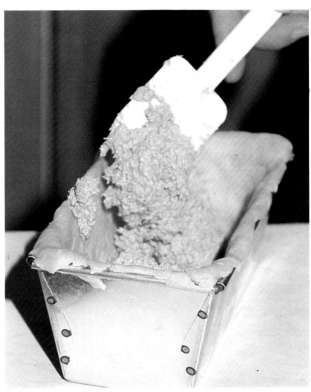

Making the duck pâté en croûte.
The photographs show slicing the breast, processing the remaining meat with the seasonings and dripping:

knuckling the pastry into the tin: adding half the duck mixture: putting in the slices of breast and sprinkling it with green peppercorns

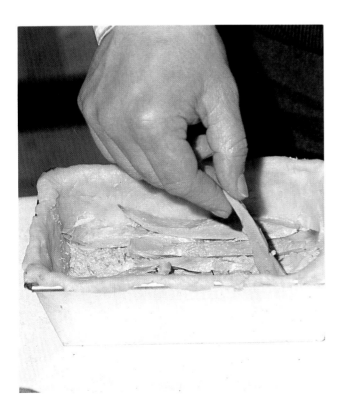

posh chicken liver pâté

This one is for a special occasion when a little light starter is just what's called for.

Double-bladed knife
8 oz (225 g) chicken livers
3 oz (75 g) butter
2 eggs
liqueur glass apple juice
salt and pepper

Defrost and drain the chicken livers. Melt 2 oz (50 g) butter in a thick sided pan and turn the livers in the melted, foaming butter for about 2 minutes, until they're brown on the outside but not hard. Put them into the bowl. Add the remaining butter to the pan, and in it scramble the 2 eggs until they are firm; add them and the small glass of apple juice to the bowl, season generously and process the whole mixture for 10 seconds. Scrape down the sides of the bowl and process for another 10 seconds until thoroughly mixed and very fine. Pour it into a white sided soufflé dish. Melt a little more butter in the pan and pour it over, running it carefully around the top to seal. Place the soufflé dish in the fridge for at least 2 hours to set before serving. This is particularly nice with hot buttered toast, for it has a lovely soft, delicate spreading consistency.

rustic chicken liver pâté

A pâté strictly to be eaten amongst friends with a taste for strong, delicious country-type foods.

Double-blade knife
3 oz (75 g) chicken livers
4 oz (100 g) chicken hearts
4 oz (100 g) butter
2 cloves garlic
juice and rind of an orange
1 teaspoon dried thyme
1 teaspoon dried tarragon
salt and pepper

Poach the chicken hearts (most butchers will supply these or use all chicken livers) in a small saucepan, generously covered with water, for 30 minutes. Remove, drain, trim off any gristly bits. Cut each heart in half, place in the bowl with the double-bladed knife. In the drained pan, melt all but 1/2 oz (13 g) of the butter until foaming. Add the chicken livers and garlic, and brown the livers until they are cooked but still slightly pink in the middle (test one to check). Add these to the bowl and rinse out the pan with the orange juice. Add that to the bowl with the grated orange rind, the herbs and seasonings. Cover and process for 20 seconds. Scrape down the sides, process again for another 10 seconds. The mixture should still have a little texture, be a bit grainy from the tiny bits of heart in the mixture. Pack it into an oval, earthenware dish and melt the last remaining butter to pour round the top as a seal. Leave it in the fridge, over-night if you can, for the flavours to blend. You can slice this pâté, or scoop it out of the bowl with a spoon. Either way, the centre of it should still be a little pink, and the flavour of the garlic and herbs should have blended thoroughly into the chicken livers.

country pâté

This is perhaps the most basic and simple of all pâtés, the kind that in restaurants is usually called 'Pâté du Chef'. That is unless the chef happens to be a master or a show off, in which case I refer you to Duck en Croûte which is coming up in a little while. But this is basically a liver pâté. It's flavoured with herbs and designed to be spread in large chunks on crusty bread. If you're putting a picnic together, take some with you, still in its terrine and use a spoon to serve it onto the bread when you get to the picnic site. A good grainy French mustard goes extremely well with this pâté, or a few dill-flavoured gherkins make a nice sharp contrast to its richness.

Double-bladed knife
1 lb (450 g) lambs liver
4 oz (100 g) beef kidney fat or suet
2 × 1 in. slices bread
1 large onion
1 teaspoon thyme
1 teaspoon oregano
2 eggs
2 bay leaves
salt and pepper

Make breadcrumbs with the bread broken into pieces, and add the peeled, quartered onion. Process until puréed. (About 10 seconds). Take it out and put it into a bowl. Into the bowl put the liver cut into 1 in. cubes, and the beef fat likewise. Process for 20 seconds. Scrape down the sides, add the thyme and oregano, a generous amount of salt and pepper, and the eggs, one at a time, while the motor is running. Switch off and add the bread and onion mixture. Process until thoroughly mixed. Pack into an oval terrine which will fit inside a baking dish and place the bay leaves on top. Fill the baking dish with water an inch deep, place the terrine in it and put the whole lot in an oven, gas mark 4, 350°F, 175°C, for 1¼ hours. You can if you like cover the top of the pâté with a sheet of foil placed lightly over it. When it's cooked and the sides have shrunk away from the terrine a little, take it out, and allow it to cool for at least 12 hours, weighted down, with a plate and a couple of 1 lb or 2 lb tins from the larder. When it's cool it'll keep in the fridge with a layer of cling-film around it for over a week, or for 4 days once it's been cut.

smoked mackerel pâté

Smoked mackerel are one of the great crafty gourmet delicacies – still about the cheapest fish we have, and yet tasting as fine, or finer, to my mind, than smoked salmon. When you are making this pâté, which has become a firm favourite in restaurants throughout the country in the last couple of years, try and choose mackerel that are not too brightly coloured but have been turned a golden brown by smoke and not bright yellow by chemical dyes. There are even some fishmongers these days who are smoking their own. Also on the market are Scandinavian style home smokers, about the size of a shoe box which produce quite the most delicious smoked fish I have ever tasted in my life.

Double-bladed knife
8 oz (225 g) smoked mackerel (fillets are fine)
4 oz (100 g) cream cheese (either fresh or Philadelphia style)
2 oz (50 g) butter
¼ teaspoon nutmeg
½ teaspoon freshly ground black pepper
1 lemon
salt and pepper

Skin and carefully bone the mackerel fillets, place them in the bowl with the cream cheese, the juice of half the lemon, the spices and seasonings. Process for 10 seconds, scrape down the bowl and process again until the mixture is thoroughly smooth and blended. Melt the butter, and with the motor running add half of it to the mixture. Switch off and pack it into attractive serving dishes. It can either be in individual ramekins for individual servings, or in a big soufflé dish for the centre of the table. Slice the other half lemon into very thin complete slices, removing any pips, and lay these in an overlapping pattern around the top of the pâté (or one single lemon slice for each ramekin). Pour the remaining melted butter over the top to seal it, and set in the fridge for at least 2 hours before serving.
Very thin brown bread and butter is traditional with this, but I must admit that hot, oven-fresh French bread is my favourite.

potted meats

Potted meats are the traditional English style pâtés which really differ from the French ones in that they happily make use of leftovers or surplus food. A piece of English frugality so often un-remarked by foreigners when judging our cooking.

All of these have a similar method, merely the contents and detailed flavourings are what makes the difference. They are also all very rich, and less of them is needed for each individual serving than pâtés.

potted turkey

Perfect for post-Christmas use of the inevitable turkey bits. Especially as the scraps that you otherwise can't find a use for go perfectly into this dish. As most people will have had their fill of turkey by the time you get round to making this, why not cover it when it's made, and put it in the freezer. A couple of months later it may prove a revelation which excites praise and smiles instead of groans and head-holding, which it might do the day after Boxing Day.

Double-bladed knife
8 oz (225 g) turkey scraps (even skin'll do though it
    shouldn't be exclusively skin)
2 or 3 tablespoons giblet stock or gravy
4 oz (100 g) butter
1/2 teaspoon salt
1/2 teaspoon black pepper
couple of tablespoons cranberry sauce (if available)
slice white bread or 2 tablespoons stuffing

Put the bread or stuffing into the bowl, process for 2 or 3 seconds until crumbed. Add the turkey scraps, all the spices and flavourings except the butter and process until a fine purée, scraping down the sides. If you haven't stock or gravy, use water because turkey is very dry. The processing should take about 15 seconds. Melt the butter, and add it, with the motor running through the feed-tube until the whole mixture is thoroughly blended. Pot in individual bowls, or in a bigger soufflé dish for general use. If serving fairly soon a small teaspoon of cranberry sauce piled in the middle with a couple of sprigs of holly makes an attractive decoration. Don't freeze it with the holly on though, it won't taste nice, and it'll make holes in the cling film!

potted tongue

If you ever cook your own tongues and slice them, hot or cold, you may find yourself with bits left over. These are perfect for this recipe, as are scraps left from shop-bought tongues, or even a 'quarter' bought specially for the purpose. There's a very meaty flavour to this recipe, and it goes especially well with old fashioned English type chutneys, or mustard a little stronger than the French care for.

Double-bladed knife
4 oz (100 g) cooked tongue
4 oz (100 g) unsalted or mildly salted butter
1/2 teaspoon each, black pepper and mustard powder
1 dessertspoon redcurrant jelly
generous pinch ground allspice

Place all the ingredients except the butter in the bowl (you can cut the tongue up if it's in large chunks), and process briefly (about 10 seconds). Melt the butter, start the motor again and pour the melted, foaming not-browned butter through the feed-tube until the mixture is thoroughly blended. Do not add any salt. The tongue, and possibly even the butter, have more than enough salt in them already. Scrape out the bowl carefully and pack the potted meat into individual ramekins or small dishes. Let it set, (it doesn't have to be in the fridge). It will keep, covered, for nearly a week.

potted cheese

Potted cheese is in fact a very old English tradition, deriving I'm sure, from our having hard cheeses which often leaves dried out remnants, these are only fit for grating, so the Continent, with its softer cheeses has never actually discovered the pleasure of this particular recipe. There's an exotic ingredient in this one as well, the mango chutney, which comes from one of Britain's other traditions – that of involving Eastern foods and flavours in its national cooking. Anyone who's ever tried a cheese and chutney sandwich and enjoyed it, is going to find this particular savoury especially succulent.

Grating disc
Double-bladed knife
8 oz (225 g) English cheese; Cheddar, Wensleydale,
    Double Gloucester or Cheshire are best (it can be old,
    and dried)
4 oz (100 g) butter
2 tablespoons mango chutney
1 teaspoon lemon juice
1/2 teaspoon black pepper
pinch cayenne pepper

Grate the cheese into the bowl, without emptying, replace the grating disc with the double-bladed mixing knife. Add the chutney and spices and the butter, softened to room temperature, but not melted and process for 10 seconds, scrape down the sides and process again. Taste, it may need a little salt if the cheese was particularly mild. You can serve this, either in ramekins like the other potted meats, or, equally attractively piled up on a pretty plate and shaped with the prongs of a fork, so that it looks rather like an old fashioned butter pat. Both its texture and taste will surprise people. And in the unlikely event of you being lucky enough to have any left over, it makes a wonderful Welsh Rarebit, melted on toast under the grill next day.

dressy dressings and super sauces

One of the nicest things about French cooking are the sauces. They almost never come out of bottles, although occasionally something that comes out of bottles goes into them. Rather, they are a blend of simple ingredients mixed with great care and skill to produce sumptuous and smooth coatings and glazes for the food. The marvellous thing about processors are that they have that skill and care, all you need are the simple ingredients and a little time.

Don't be afraid to experiment with the sauces. In Britain our classic cauliflower with cheese sauce, or, if you're from the North, leeks with white sauce, seems to be about our limit. But, in France, you might get carrots in a *béchamel* sauce flavoured with caraway seeds, broad beans in a rich parsley sauce, or hard-boiled eggs covered in a creamy onion sauce and browned under the grill. Enjoy yourself, the world of super sauces is at your finger tips, and you need hardly more time to make them than it takes to read about it.

The crafty cook makes mayonnaise

dressings

In Britain, only too often, we tend to regard salad cream as the be all and end all of salad dressings. While I have nothing against salad cream, I do think there are a lot of rather more exciting things to put on your lettuce. Some of the ideas of what sort of salads you might put them on are on pages 44-50 in the Salad section. But for the moment here are some rather unusual ideas on dressings that could probably go on most lettuce, cucumber, beetroot and tomato salads without having to explore the realms of exotic ingredients.

lemon dressing

This is my version of what's known variously as *vinaigrette* or French dressing. It's a flavour combination that comes from the Middle East where they eat an enormous variety and range of salads. The lemon juice is lighter than vinegar in similar recipes, and has the other great advantage of not destroying any flavours in other foods you might be eating the salad with.

Double-bladed knife
1/2 cup salad oil
1/4 cup lemon juice (fresh, or bottled is fine)
1/2 teaspoon mustard powder
1/2 teaspoon salt
1 teaspoon sugar

Put all the ingredients, except the oil, into the bowl and process for 3 to 5 seconds. Take out the plastic pusher and pour in the oil in a steady stream. The dressing will thicken quite dramatically and to a lovely single-cream consistency. It will coat each leaf of a lettuce, or tenderly clasp a tomato's blushing cheeks.
A variation on this dressing which is becoming increasingly popular abroad, but very rarely tried here is garlic and herbs. Start by finely chopping 2 peeled and quartered cloves of garlic and a handful of herbs (parsley, basil and watercress seem to be the favourites). Then add the lemon juice and seasonings and proceed as above. It's not a dish for people who don't like garlic or who aren't well acquainted. But for those who do and are, it's almost good enough to eat on its own, dipping hot crusty French bread into it.

blue cheese

This is an American dressing which is normally made in expensive restaurants with great flamboyance by a head waiter standing at your side, and mashing the cheese up with a silver fork to begin the operation. It may look good, but it doesn't taste anything like as good as the processor product. There is no silver fork wielded by a Maitre D. that ever managed to get the blend of smoothness and sharpness achieved by your friendly electric chef.

Double-bladed knife
6 oz (150 g) blue cheese
coffee cup of milk
1/2 teaspoon made mustard
1/4 pint (150 ml) oil
1/2 teaspoon granulated sugar
1 tablespoon lemon juice

Crumble the blue cheese roughly and add it with the milk to the bowl and process for about 5 seconds. Scrape down the sides and add mustard, sugar and the lemon juice if you like your dressings really sharp. Put the lid on, switch on, remove the plastic pusher and pour in the oil in a slight steady stream. It should never go in all at once, but be added gradually. As the oil is added you will notice a change in the noise of the motor and the blades will slow down suddenly as the dressing becomes thick. The more oil you add, the thicker is becomes. I like it just this side of softly whipped double cream. Try it with your regular salads, or with quarters of the American Ice-berg or Webbs Wonder style lettuce, washed but left whole in the head. Almost a meal in itself.

mayonnaise

Said to have been invented in honour of one of Napoleon's victories, the history of this sauce goes back a lot further than the early nineteenth century. Traditionally one of the most difficult and skill-requiring sauces of all to make, with oil being added drop by drop, the egg yolks being beaten by hand with a wooden spoon, – it is now, thanks to electricity, one of the easiest and quickest to make at home. Have courage, and if it does go wrong and curdle, by some accident or mistake, simply pour it out of the bowl, add another egg, and add the curdled mixture like the oil in the recipe below – you'll just have twice as much mayonnaise at the end, that's all.

Double-bladed knife
1 whole egg
½ teaspoon salt
½ teaspoon granulated sugar
2 teaspoons lemon juice
½ teaspoon made French mustard
8 fl oz (250 ml) salad oil

Put the egg, mustard, salt, sugar and lemon juice into a bowl. Cover and process for 10 seconds. Add a quarter of the oil and process for another 5 seconds. Remove the plastic pusher and pour in the rest of the oil gradually with the engine running, in a slow, steady stream. The engine note will suddenly change as the mayonnaise thickens. You can go on adding oil with the mayonnaise getting thicker as you go.

You can double the quantities if you wish and you may find you have to if you own one of the big capacity processors. The mayonnaise, which has a lovely light lemony flavour will keep perfectly well in reasonably large quantities in the fridge if well covered.

green mayonnaise

A variation is to blend a generous handful of green herbs, parsley, young spinach leaves, chives or a little sorrel, are the favourite candidates. Process for 10 seconds before the mayonnaise is made. Once the mayonnaise has thickened, stop the motor, add the herbs which you have reserved, scrape down the sides, switch on again, adding a little more oil, and turn out your *mayonnaise* or *sauce verte* which is used not only as a salad dressing but as a delicious accompaniment to cold beef or tongue.

Cracking the egg for mayonnaise into the bowl

Dripping in the oil while processor is working

béchamel or white sauce (and variations)

This is the basic sauce of French cooking. It's one of those sauces that, if it's right, is absolutely delicious, and if it's wrong, is a lumpy nightmare. It's the basis of some of the most delicious dishes in the world – and with a processor it's just not possible to get it to come out lumpy.

Double-bladed knife
1½ tablespoons softened butter
1½ tablespoons flour
½ pint (300 ml) milk
pinch salt
pinch ground nutmeg

Make sure the butter is soft, almost to the point of being runny. Add the butter, flour, salt and nutmeg to the bowl; pour in the milk and process for 10 seconds. Tip the whole mixture into a saucepan (non-stick is best, it helps with the washing up and you don't waste any of the sauce). Stir over a medium heat until the sauce thickens and goes shiny. Turn the heat down and allow to simmer 4 or 5 minutes to make sure the flour is all cooked through. This is basic *béchamel* or white sauce. Variations are endless, but here are some of the best: –

Béchamel or white sauce: place 1½ tablespoons flour in the bowl

sauce mornay

Put 6 oz (150 g) of cheese through the grating disc and after the sauce has cooked for 4 minutes, stir it in over a low heat. When melted, stir again and allow to settle for 1 minute over the lowest possible heat. This the French call *Sauce Mornay*, and is delicious used on fish, but will enoble even one of our humble cauliflowers.

sauce soubise (onion sauce)

Cook a finely sliced onion in another half a tablespoonful of butter until it's soft but not coloured. After making the *béchamel* stir the onion in and simmer very slowly for 5 minutes to allow the flavours to become infused. *Sauce soubise*, is delicious with sausages, or poured over hard-boiled eggs then glazed under the grill.

parsley sauce

For a classic English parsley sauce start by putting a good handful of parsley heads and broad stalks into the processor bowl. Process for 5 seconds, scrape the sides down and process for another 5 seconds or until the parsley is super finely chopped. Scrape out into a bowl and keep. Make the *béchamel*, and just before serving add the chopped parsley and a squeeze of lemon juice.

Process for 10 seconds or until smooth

Add 1¹/2 tablespoons soft butter, and a pinch of ground nutmeg or a scraping of whole nutmeg

Pour in ¹/2 a pint of milk

Pour the mixture into a saucepan

Gently heat, stirring all the time

sauce béarnaise

This is the French sauce for red meats. It's supposed to have been James Bond's favourite with steak. Certainly *Chateaubriand* with *sauce béarnaise* is one of the classic dishes of haute cuisine. But, if you're feeling the pinch a bit towards the end of the week, it's quite nice with hamburgers too. It's amazing what a transformation a little special touch like that can make to an everyday family meal.

Double-bladed knife
1 small onion
2 tablespoons wine or tarragon vinegar
1 egg
1 egg yolk
4 oz (100 g) unsalted or lightly salted butter
½ teaspoon golden French mustard

Chop the onion very finely, scrape out and add to the vinegar in a small saucepan. Bring to the boil and cook until the vinegar is reduced by half. Combine the egg, egg yolk and the mustard in the bowl, and process for 3 seconds. Melt the butter in a separate saucepan and with the motor running pour it, foaming, but not brown, into the egg mixture. Process for 3 or 4 seconds until smooth and then add to the onion and vinegar reduction. Stir until blended and heat through over a medium to low flame until the mixture thickens. Like *hollandaise*, it's fairly close relative, this sauce shouldn't be kept waiting much more than 10 minutes.

hollandaise

Despite its Dutch name this is another French sauce. Particularly delicious with fish and light dishes especially chicken ones. It's a sauce which traditionally takes 20 minutes and total concentration, however, with a processor it only takes 2 minutes from scratch.

Double-bladed knife
1 egg
1 egg yolk
4 oz (100 g) unsalted or lightly salted butter
teaspoon lemon juice
salt and pepper

Cut the butter into chunks and melt it in a small saucepan until it foams but *does not* turn brown. Combine the egg, yolk, lemon juice, a pinch of salt and pepper, in the bowl and process for 5 seconds then, with the machine on, carefully pour the foaming butter in through the feed-tube. Process for 3 seconds until smooth. Tip the mixture into the saucepan and reheat over a low heat until the mixture suddenly thickens. Stop cooking it at this point or it will become fancy scrambled eggs! It can be kept warm for up to 10 minutes without any major harm coming to it, but should be eaten quickly and as fresh as possible; delicious on poached salmon, or even just new potatoes. It has an incomparable delicate flavour.

sauce maltaise

A variation is to add a tablespoon of blood-orange juice instead of the lemon juice when making it. This produces a pink coloured *hollandaise* with an orange flavour and is known as *Sauce Maltaise*, after the island where the oranges are supposed to have originated. It's particularly nice with asparagus.

tomato sauce

Also known in France as a *tomato coulis*, this is really a sauce which Italy claims by right. At its worst it can be a nasty oily preparation, but at its best it's one of the most versatile of all sauces, to be eaten on its own with some freshly cooked pasta and grated parmesan.

Double-bladed knife
1 medium sized onion
1 clove garlic
4 tablespoons oil (olive, sunflower or peanut)
16 oz (450 g) tin Italian or Bulgarian tomatoes
1/2 teaspoon basil
1/2 teaspoon oregano
1 desertspoon butter
1/2 teaspoon sugar
salt and pepper

Peel and cut the onion into quarters. Process with the peeled clove of garlic until finely chopped. Scrape out into a saucepan in which you've heated the oil, and fry gently until soft and golden. Add the tin of tomatoes, breaking the fruit open gently with a wooden spoon. Add the sugar, salt and pepper. Simmer gently for 25 minutes, with a lid on the saucepan held open by a wooden spoon. Pour the mixture into the bowl (which it wasn't necessary to wash) and process for 5 seconds. Scrape the sides of the bowl down; add the butter and herbs and process 3 seconds more until the sauce is smooth but still has some texture left. It can be stored before use in the fridge in sealed containers or kept in the deep freeze.

salads and crudités

In Britain I think we are often caught between the upper and the nether millstones as far as our salads are concerned. For first courses the French have a wonderful way with what they call *crudités* – raw vegetables, dressed in a variety of ways that we'd look on as salads but which they serve as *hors d'oeuvres*. In the field of main course salads the Americans have the best of it, with a series of quite amazing dishes – meals on their own. Although they vary the ingredients dramatically they manage to combine a freshness, a balance of flavours, and really rich dressings, with extraordinarily attractive presentation.

In this chapter, I have therefore concentrated on these two groups which I think can teach us all something. There's a section on French crudités, and a section on American fancy salads. Do, by the way, try the one with strawberries and cucumbers; it may sound outlandish, but until you have tried it you just don't know what the perfect accompaniment to a summer's day (or poached salmon) can be.

A table laid with salads and crudités

coleslaw plain and simple

Worldwide, coleslaw is the most famous of all American salads. Fundamentally, as it's name implies, it's a shredded cabbage salad, and this is the basic and original kind, made just with cabbage, and a few additions to add flavour.

The best dressing of all is a mixture of mayonnaise and a little French or lemon dressing. There are alternatives you can buy in the grocer's – Hellman's Mayonnaise (a real American kind), or coleslaw dressings made by firms like Kraft, – but whatever you do, please, please have the courage to avoid using salad cream. The dressings on pages 36-39 are easily made in the processor, but salad cream really will destroy the natural balance of flavours that exists even in this simple example of the American salad art.

Slicing disc and shredding disc
1 firm white Dutch-type cabbage
2 carrots
1 eating apple
1 cup mayonnaise (page 39)
1/2 cup lemon dressing (page 38) (or equivalent of shop-
    bought coleslaw dressings)

Cut the cabbage into quarters or eighths, depending on the size, so that it will fit through the feed-tube. Fit the slicing disc and put the cabbage through it. Change to the grating disc, and grate the peeled carrots and the cored, unpeeled but quartered apple. Stir it all round; tip it into a serving bowl; add the lemon dressing and then stir in the mayonnaise. This is basic coleslaw; although you can if you wish, dress it up a little with a sprinkling of freshly chopped parsley over the top. It improves if made about an hour or two before eating and then left in the fridge for the flavours to blend.

bread salad

In the Middle East they have a rather more generous view of what makes a good salad, than we tend to in Europe. Bread, after all, is not the first thing that springs to mind. But this is not only a delicious recipe, it is also extremely economical. Until you've tasted the salad, you must not try and adjust the seasonings though to Western tastes. It may seem too lemony; but when you taste it you will find the balance actually does work, terribly well. Once again without a processor it's a salad that requires a great deal of work and effort.

Double-bladed knife
6 thick slices of white bread
bunch of spring onions
8 oz (225 g) tomatoes
good size bunch of parsley
8 radishes
the heart of a cos lettuce
4 tablespoons salad oil
6 tablespoons lemon juice
1 desertspoon sugar
1 teaspoon salt

Put the parsley into the bowl and process until finely chopped add the oil, lemon juice, sugar, salt, washed and trimmed radishes, quartered tomatoes, and trimmed spring onions. Process until thoroughly blended and the vegetables are chopped into fairly small flakes. Pour into a bowl and without washing the bowl or blade, put in the slices of bread, broken into rough chunks and process until fine breadcrumbs, you may have to scrape the bowl down a couple of times. Add 1/2 cup of water and process again for 3 seconds to mix thoroughly. Take out and mix the breadcrumbs and the vegetable dressing. Taste for seasoning, it may need a little more liquid in which case add up to another cup of water to moisten the breadcrumbs. Line a dish with the inner leaves of a cos lettuce and fill the centre with the bread salad.

Bread salad

Waldorf salad

waldorf salad

This is one of those meals in a salad bowl that the Americans are so good at. It's a lovely creamy mixture of chicken, celery and walnuts, in a rather special mayonnaise.

Slicing disc
Double-bladed knife
1 lb (450 g) boned cooked chicken meat
6 sticks of celery
3 oz (75 g) walnuts
3 eating apples – preferably with different coloured skins red and green
8 fl oz (250 ml) of mayonnaise – home made is the nicest
(see page 39)

Take an ounce of the walnuts, put them into the processor with the mayonnaise and process for 10 seconds, scrape the sides down and process again until the walnuts are really finely chopped, and look like little tiny specs in the mayonnaise. (If you are making mayonnaise from scratch you can start by processing the walnuts until they are finely ground, then add the egg.) Without emptying the bowl change the double-bladed knife for the slicing disc. Wash and trim the celery and pack it vertically into the feed-tube, slice it into the bowl, followed by the apples, quartered and cored but not peeled (the coloured skins are particularly attractive in the dish.) Cut the chicken meat into neat 1/4 in. cubes and without processing it add to the bowl. Stir thoroughly and pile into a serving dish lined with cos lettuce leaves. Decorate with the remaining 2 oz (50 g) of shelled walnuts halved. And when you serve it make sure everyone gets their share of the nuts.

salad elana

One of the more exotic and exciting salads, this combines cucumber and strawberries with an orange flavoured dressing. Extraordinary though it may sound, even the black pepper sprinkled on the salad has a tradition in strawberry eating going back many years. Do try it, the combination is surprisingly delicate and delicious, and a wonderful accompaniment to almost all kinds of summer fish, and to poached, fresh salmon in particular. We can afford, or find, salmon and strawberries very rarely, but do put them together if you can, even if it's only once a year.

Slicing disc
1/2 cucumber
8 oz (225 g) large firm strawberries
8 tablespoons orange juice
2 tablespoons oil
1 teaspoon sugar
1 teaspoon salt

Score the cucumber with the prongs of a fork, all the way round in an even pattern. Top and tail it, and slice it, holding it carefully upright, through the slicing disc. Scoop out the cucumber, sprinkle it with salt and put it to drain in a colander for 30 minutes. Hull and wash the strawberries, keeping aside any that are not at least an inch across for decoration later. Put the large strawberries carefully into the feed-tube and slice, using only the weight of the plastic pusher to push the strawberries through lest they become squashed. Arrange the drained and rinsed cucumber in overlapping concentric circles on a shallow dish. Lay the strawberry slices around in an equally pretty pattern, saving the smaller ones for decoration at the centre of the dish. Mix the orange juice, oil, salt and sugar (this can be done in the processor in advance, if you wish, using the double-bladed knife). Pour over the salad, making sure to coat both strawberries and cucumber thoroughly; and just before serving, screw a little fresh ground black pepper over the whole dish. The result is not only delicious, it is also extremely pretty.

The colourful and unusual salad elana. The photographs opposite show the cucumber being scored and then sliced, then the strawberries being sliced and finally the two being arranged on a plate

chinese cabbage salad

Although the title of this suggests an Eastern origin, in fact it's a salad that I've developed, using that marvellously adaptable Chinese vegetable, a cross between a cos and a savoy cabbage, that's so widely available in the shops in Britain these days. One of the essentials for the success of this salad is to make sure that its really very finely sliced, a processor, of course, making it really easy. The addition of the red pepper, makes a spectacular difference to the appearance of this salad.

Do use olive oil in the dressing, – normally I don't bother, but on this occasion it is worth making the special effort. The tastes of the fruity oil, the crisp greenness of the salad and the rich slightly peppery flavour of the pimento, make it a very special combination indeed. Especially nice and surprising to serve at a winter dinner party when no one is expecting anything quite so fresh and attractive.

Slicing disc
Double-bladed knife
1 Chinese cabbage
1 red pepper
3 tablespoons olive oil
1/2 teaspoon sugar
pinch salt
2 tablespoons lemon juice

Cut the cabbage into quarters, lengthwise, take out the heart section at the bottom, and if it's the right size place each quarter into the feed-tube and slice down. If it's still too big you may only need half of the cabbage to feed four people, then cut it into eighths and slice it vertically through the feed-tube so you get very thin ribbons. Take out and pile into a bowl, white china is very pretty with the shades of green that the cabbage produces sliced like this. Cut the pepper in half, take out the seeds, pack the halves inside each other and slice those through the disc as well. Spread the pepper slices over the top of the cabbage. Change to the double-bladed knife put the dressing ingredients into the bowl and process to mix. Just before serving pour the dressing over the salad, don't toss it until you actually serve it, as that will disturb the prettiness of the colours and destroy one of the pleasures of this, my favourite winter salad. (If you don't eat it all at once, it will survive if kept quietly in the fridge, for about another 12 hours).

florida fruit plate

A straight steal this, from the most expensive hotel on the Miami Beach. My first real experience of the different way that Americans in general and Floridians, in particular, treat fruit and vegetables when they're turning out a salad. Do make sure that each ingredient is kept just a little bit separate and set up really decoratively around the plate. I'm going to suggest a series of ingredients but you can modify them to suit your purse and the availability in the shops.

For two people the ingredients are:

Slicing disc
Double-bladed knife
1 avocado
bunch of radishes
1 peach
1 small punnet of strawberries
2 apples
1 pear
bunch of white grapes
3 sprigs of mint
1 carton of sour cream or plain yoghurt
1 carton of banana yoghurt
lemon juice
salt and pepper

Halve the avocado, remove the stone, and peel it carefully. Cut each half lengthwise, into 1/4 in. strips without severing the butt end of the avocado completely, and gently spread each half into a fan. Put in the centre of an oval plate and sprinkle over some lemon juice. Halve but don't peel the apples, core them and slice into the bowl. Dip them into a little lemon juice, to stop them going brown and arrange them also in fan shapes, around the plate. Wash and trim the radishes and slice them having packed them all into the feed-tube first. Halve and stone the peach and slice that. Keep the strawberries whole, peel and core the pear, cut it in half and slice that lengthwise. Arrange all the fruit in attractive patterns, around the avocados. Garnishing with the grapes and radishes and mint sprigs. Change to the double-bladed knife and process the sour cream, yoghurt and seasonings until amalgamated. Spoon a little dressing over each avocado and pass the rest in a sauce boat.

crudités

Crudités aren't really that crude but the French word for raw vegetables. They are all basically a single vegetable, treated and dressed in a particular way. Don't be afraid to experiment yourself; the ones here are just suggestions, although I think you'll find that they make what we regard as very ordinary, common or garden vegetables into something that looks and tastes special. Indeed, one of the pleasures of crudités, is the rediscovering of the real flavour of things we have been taking for granted for a long time. Eat a combination of 3 or 4 as a first course.

beetroot and yoghurt

This most despised of salad vegetables takes on a really new flavour served and dressed this way. If you grow your own beetroot it's certainly worth boiling them for this dish, but ordinary shop-bought, ready-cooked beetroot are fine. A hint, by the way, for peeling cooked beetroot. If you find the skins difficult to get off, try doing it under water, for some reason they come off far more easily without tearing up the surface of the vegetable.

Grating disc
8 oz (225 g) peeled, boiled beets
1 tablespoon lemon juice
1 tablespoon salad oil
pinch sugar
1 small carton plain yoghurt
salt

Grate the beetroots into the bowl. Stir in the lemon juice, oil and sugar, and a good seasoning of salt. Leave to stand in a bowl in the fridge for the flavours to penetrate. Serve with a large spoonful of yoghurt, stirred, at the last minute into the middle of each individual serving, or piled high in the middle of the bowl of beetroot. You'll be amazed at the texture, as well as the flavour, of this dish.

minted cucumber

Sliced cucumber should hardly need an introduction to this country where it was immortalised in tiny brown bread and butter sandwiches with their crusts cut off; but although the French also slice it up, they treat it in rather a different manner.

Slicing disc
1 whole cucumber
sprig of fresh mint
1 teaspoon salt
4 tablespoons natural yoghurt

Hold the cucumber carefully in your left hand and, taking a fork with sharp, firm prongs, run them down the length of the cucumber. Turn the cucumber round until all sides of it are thoroughly scored. This serves 2 purposes, both to help the cucumber drain itself of excess liquid, and also to provide an extremely pretty pattern when it's sliced across. To achieve this, place the cucumber upright in the feed-tube with the slicing disc in position. Switch on and feed the cucumber in by hand until it vanishes into the tube; finish with the plastic pusher. Switch off and you will find a whole series of very fine cucumber flowers. Mix the salt with these and put them to drain in a colander for half an hour to get rid of the excess liquid. Bury the sprig of mint in the middle of the cucumber piled into a serving dish. Just before serving, take out the mint and stir in the yoghurt. You can serve it without the draining of the cucumber, but it very rapidly becomes watery, even just sitting on the table for 5 minutes.

carrots with meux mustard

Carrots in France are usually associated with Vichy, down towards the South West, where the spring water that they are supposed to be best cooked in comes from. There's a recipe for Carrots Vichy further on, see page 81, but this recipe is associated with a town a bit further north called Meux where that lovely crunchy French mustard with lots of bits in it is made. For the dressing you can use bought mayonnaise, or, easiest of all, use the processed mayonnaise from page 39, adding the mustard as directed in the recipe.

Double-bladed knife
Grating disc
1 lb (450 g) carrots
8 tablespoons mayonnaise
1½ tablespoons Meux 'whole grain' mustard
small bunch parsley

Chop the parsley, scrape it out of the bowl and reserve. Fit the grating disc, peel the carrots and trim them so that they fit into the feed-tube lying on their sides lengthwise. This is in order to produce long curling slivers of carrots, rather than short, blunt ones. It doesn't make much difference to the taste, but a lot to the appearance of this dish. Grate all the carrots in the same manner. Mix the mustard and mayonnaise together, and turn the carrot slivers firmly in this until all are well coated. Transfer into a serving dish and sprinkle with the parsley. This does not need to be kept very long before it is eaten, although it will do perfectly well in the fridge for up to 6 hours.

celery and walnut

This is a flavour combination that comes from a part of the heart of France where walnut trees are so common they even press oil from the nuts and use it as a salad dressing. If you can find any, and are rich enough to afford it, it makes a wonderful addition to this recipe. If not, ordinary oil will do, and ordinary walnuts; the more white the celery though, the better, as the green, rather stringy variety really doesn't go terribly well in this recipe.

Slicing disc
1 head celery
2 oz (50 g) shelled walnuts
4 tablespoons oil
2 tablespoons lemon juice
1 teaspoon Dijon mustard

Wash and clean the celery, stripping off all the leaves, but retaining those from the heart section. Pack the celery sticks tightly into the feed-tube, switch on and push the celery sticks down evenly so they all slice across the grain. Stop the motor and repeat until all the celery is used up. Break up the shelled walnut halves by hand, and crumble them over the celery in a bowl (retaining 1 or 2 for decoration). Mix the oil, mustard and lemon juice together; dress the celery and walnuts; decorate with the whole walnut halves, and allow 20 minutes for the flavours to blend.

A selection of crudités — celery and walnut, beetroot and yoghurt, and carrots with meux mustard

A nest of fresh country eggs

eggs are exciting

The most used and probably the least respected of foods is the egg. If you think about it, whatever your style of cooking, often one of the absolutely essential ingredients is an egg. Yet, egg and chips is almost a symbol of not bothering, and a dish based on eggs is something few of us would really consider except as a standby or a cheap family meal. I hope that what follows may change that. You may well ask what difference does a processor make to eggs, because with the best will in the world, they don't have to be beaten electrically, although the difference a really smooth, thorough beating makes, I think, is quite remarkable. What it does is allow you to add flavour, introduce texture, blend in other ingredients, and generally transform a common or at least *country* garden egg into the realms of grand food.

caroline's cheese pudding

Soufflés have always been a matter of great mystery to me. It's not that I can't make them, I'm just not quite sure why anyone bothers, because they always seem to be so insubstantial that one goes chasing after them rather like clouds, never quite catching up with either their texture or taste. This dish is a primitive soufflé, taught me by an old friend called Caroline, the lady of the title. While there's nothing insubstantial about this dish, either in its texture or its flavours, the ingredients must make it one of the cheapest family favourites on record.

Grating disc
Double-bladed knife
2 thick slices of bread (stale is OK as long as it's not rock hard)
4 oz (100 g) cheese
2 eggs
½ pint (300 ml) milk

Grate the cheese into the bowl; take it out and keep it. Change to the double-bladed knife. Put in the bread, broken into chunks, process until fine breadcrumbs. Take them out and mix these lightly with the cheese. Separate the eggs and add the yolks to the bowl (which doesn't need to be washed) with the milk and a generous seasoning of salt and pepper. Process for about 3 seconds until thoroughly mixed, add to the breadcrumbs and cheese mixture and then whip the whites with a beater until stiff but not grainy. Mix these carefully into the pudding and pile it all into a buttered baking dish with the sides at least an inch higher than the mixture before it's cooked. Put it into a medium oven, gas mark 5, 375°F, 190°C, for approximately 45 minutes, until a skewer or sharp knife, slid into the middle comes out clean. It'll rise, though not so spectactularly as a true soufflé, the top will go brown and bubbly and there will be a delicious cheesy smell coming from the oven. Resist eating it until the skewer comes out clean, and then eat it quickly, with perhaps a green salad, or some fruit to follow it.

Variation; A variation that I'm particularly fond of, although Caroline hasn't authorised it, is to add a handful of chopped, *fresh* herbs (use the double-bladed knife to chop them, of course), parsley, marjoram and chives are my favourites for this. The herbs stay green, and add a lovely fresh, country flavour to the whole pudding. Dried herbs just don't seem to work quite so well.

Making the cheese pudding: adding the milk to the egg yolks

Pouring the milk mixture onto the breadcrumbs and cheese

Adding the stiffly beaten egg whites

Smoothing the pudding in a dish before baking to a golden brown

egg mousse

A very crafty starter this, made from ingredients you can keep easily in the fridge and in the store cupboard. Don't let on how easily it's made though because that would give the game away, and one of the pleasures of crafty cooking is that people think that far more effort is involved than actually is. That way, they get to feel cosseted and you get to put your feet up. The perfect combination!

Double-bladed knife
3 hard-boiled eggs
2 spring onions or small sprig of chives
1 teaspoon lemon juice
1 tin consommé (it must be one that can be served cold as a jelly)
6 tablespoons mayonnaise – home made is best (see page 39)

Melt the consommé gently but do not bring to the boil, add the lemon juice and reserve. Chop the green and white parts of the spring onions or the chives in the bowl then without taking the herbs out add the halved hard-boiled eggs and process for 5 seconds until chopped. Scrape down the sides of the bowl, add the consommé which should be cool, and the mayonnaise. Process all together for another 3–5 seconds until thoroughly mixed. Pour the whole mixture, when you have tasted it for seasoning, into a soufflé dish, and put in the fridge to chill for at least 2 hours. The consommé should set completely before you serve it. It's nicest spooned out of the dish and eaten with wholemeal or granary toast. The eggs should be left in large enough pieces to give a little bit of bite to the otherwise smooth and creamy mousse.

smoked salmon scramble

Another example of how processors make a little luxury go a long way, is this trick with smoked salmon. I use it as a favourite starter for special parties; in which case serve it either on a carefully stamped out toast round (crusts removed and cut with one of those crinkly-edged cutters) or piled into the smallest, most delicate china bowls you've got. Either way, it's definitely 'ooh and ahh' time. And for a personal treat, when there's no one else around, it's not only delicious but extremely quick – and you don't have to cut the toast in fancy ways.

Double-bladed knife
2 oz (50 g) smoked salmon
6 eggs
1 tablespoon lemon juice
2 oz (50 g) butter
1 tablespoon processor chopped parsley
salt and pepper

Many shops that sell smoked salmon have packages of cheap off-cuts which are fine for this, as it's the flavour, not the long, thin slices, that matter.
Keep aside 2 or 3 slivers of smoked salmon, and add the rest to the bowl with the eggs and seasonings (but not the parsley). Process for 5 seconds, scrape down the sides and process again until the smoked salmon is chopped extremely finely into the egg mixture. Melt the butter, but please don't be stingy with it, the quantity is important, in a thick saucepan. When it's melted, but not browned at all, add the eggs and scramble gently stirring with a wooden spoon, until they are soft and creamy but not set hard, they will go on cooking when you take them off the heat. Pile them either onto the buttered toast rounds or into small china ramekins, or even giant egg cups. Sprinkle the parsley on the top, decorate with the reserved smoked salmon pieces and serve quickly while it's still piping hot.

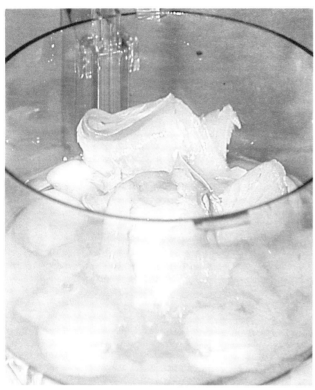

For the smoked salmon scramble: place the eggs, seasonings and smoked salmon in the bowl

Carefully pour the processed mixture into a hot saucepan

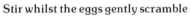

Stir whilst the eggs gently scramble

The crafty cook enjoying the scramble

Breaking the eggs for the spanish omelette into the
processor bowl

Gently frying and turning the potato, onion and salami
mixture

Pouring in the processed eggs before turning the heat
down and leaving the omelette to set as shown on the
opposite page

spanish omelette

Spanish omelettes are my family's favourite and an absolute essential part of Saturday lunchtime. This is not least because of a crafty desire to use up leftovers, and all the bits and pieces that get stuck in the fridge during the week and are still in a fit state to be consumed, often find their way into this particular dish. It is possible however, to use special ingredients for it, which turns it into an especially good tasting and visually attractive dish, but if next Saturday lunchtime you happen to have a few bits and pieces, don't be afraid to try. It's best served, straight from the frying pan it's cooked in, (placed on a mat on the table) in large wedges rather like a cake, and I find crusty wholemeal bread, lots of butter and cheese and fruit to follow, make a good enough meal for the most hungry of families.

Double-bladed knife
Slicing disc
1/2 lb (225 g) cooked potatoes
1 onion
4 oz (100 g) mixed, frozen vegetables
2 oz (50 g) salami or similar cooked, cold meat
1 tomato
8 eggs
2 tablespoons oil
1 oz (25 g) butter
salt and pepper

Put the peeled, quartered onion and the salami or cold meat into the bowl and process until coarsely chopped. Replace the knife with the slicing disc and slice into the mixture the cold boiled potatoes. Take a large 10 to 12 in. frying pan, put in a couple of tablespoons of oil and fry the potato mixture gently until the onions are softened and the whole has a few flecks of crisp brown. Turn it over regularly. After 3 or 4 minutes add the frozen vegetables (they can be still frozen) and cook them with the mixture for another 3 minutes. Put the eggs and seasoning, into the bowl and process for 3 or 4 seconds. Turn the pan heat up to hot, add a small nob of butter, and pour in the eggs, scrambling and mixing the whole panful together until the eggs start to set. Turn the heat down and leave until it's cooked through (about 4 minutes). Before serving slice the tomato thinly and place it in ring patterns on the egg.
Sausage variation:
1/2 lb (225 g) sausages
A variation and one that stretches 1/2 lb (225 g) of sausages to feed 4 people, is to start by frying the sausages carefully until they are cooked through and brown, but not burst and burnt. Proceed as above leaving out the salami and when the omelette's almost set, put in the the sausages cut in half lengthwise, like spokes in a wheel, and arrange the tomato slices between them. A favourite with the children, this one; and pretty good for their parties too.

Welsh honey roast lamb served on a bed of potatoes, carrots and onions

something special food for parties

This is a chapter of very special dishes, which a processor makes such light work of. They come in all shapes and sizes, from quick-fry Italian style chops to marinated and baked chicken dishes from Kashmir. What they have in common, apart from being helped by the new crafty kitchen tool and tasting delicious, is that they all do rather well for special occasions; the dinner party for particularly close friends, that special tête-a-tête, or the night the Committee Chairman comes to dinner. The other thing is that they are all main courses, designed for four, or if it says so specifically, six people.

The important thing with dishes like this is to choose a menu to go with them that's simple and balances well. For the crispy fried things a soup or a creamy pâté to start with; for the creamy things, a crumbly salad and a fruity pudding. If you're planning a special dinner it's always a good idea to try and get as much done in advance as possible. A processor of course helps with this enormously, but even then, try and make sure that you only have one dish to actually cook and work at when the guests arrive, and that way *you* can enjoy the evening too.

welsh honey roast lamb

Honey and lamb, not really such a strange combination when you think about the way we already regard redcurrant jelly, or apple sauce as natural accompaniments to meat. In Wales, like, strangely enough in China, they have long used a thin coating of runny honey on meat to provide a crisp caramelised surface. This is really a very easy dish on the cook because it's all done, meat and vegetables, in the one pan – another example of the knowledge our ancestors had about cooking which unfortunately we seem to have lost. What our forebears didn't have was the processor, and I think you'll find that in this recipe, as in so many others, it'll make a lot of difference saving you time and trouble, whilst adding to the flavour of the final dish.

Slicing disc
1 shoulder lamb
4 tablespoons runny honey
1 lb (450 g) potatoes
8 oz (225 g) onions
1 lb (450 g) carrots

Peel or scrub the potatoes, depending on how old they are. Peel the carrots and the onions, and cut them so that they will just fit into the feed-tube. Put in the slicing disc, feed through all three vegetables until you have a mixture of onion, carrot and potato in the mixing bowl. Take this out and place it in the bottom of a baking dish large enough to hold the whole of the shoulder of lamb. If you are fond of garlic you can at this stage insert a couple of slivers into the skin of the lamb. Place the lamb on top of the vegetables, put the dish in a pre-heated oven on the rack over the baking tray at mark 5, 375°F, 190°C and roast it for 30 minutes. Slide the lamb out of the oven and spread the runny honey on it. Put it back immediately and allow to cook for another 17–20 minutes per lb, depending on whether you like your lamb rare or not. The juices from the meat and the honey drip down onto the vegetables and make the most delicious savoury bake to go with the crisply cooked and juicy lamb. It's a country dish this, but very much one for special and joyful occasions.

tandoori chicken

Already a firm favourite with the more sophisticated take-aways, Tandoori chicken is a dish that comes from the North of India on the Kashmiri/Punjab border. It was supposed to have reached its perfection at the courts of the Mogul emperors in Delhi, but it's possible, especially with a processor and a modern oven, to make a very passable copy.

Slicing disc
Double-bladed knife
a whole chicken, skinned and cut up into portion sized
    pieces
16 fl oz plain yoghurt
1 tablespoon Tandoori spice or curry powder
2 cloves garlic
1 large onion
if possible, a small handful of fresh mint

Peel and quarter the onion, and slice it into the bowl. Remove the onion and replace the slicing disc with the double-bladed knife. Add the peeled and quartered garlic, the mint (if used), the yoghurt and the spices, – use either the Tandoori mix or the curry powder, not both. Process for 10 seconds, scrape down the sides of the bowl and process again for another 3 seconds. Place the skinned chicken in a glass or china mixing bowl. Pour the onion, yoghurt and spice mixture over the top, turn it until thoroughly coated and leave in the fridge for a minimum of 2 hours; up to 12 hours is possible for a really deeply flavoured chicken. Take out of the bowl, shake the excess yoghurt mixture off and discard it. Place the pieces of chicken on a rack over a baking tray in a hot mark 6, 400°F, 200°C oven, and bake for 30 minutes or until crisp and brown on the outside and cooked through. Serve with Indian breads (or the Greek *pitta* bread), fresh yoghurt mixed with a little cucumber, mango chutney and a salad made of onion rings and tomato chunks. Encourage your guests to eat it with their fingers, it's quite the nicest way to get the best of the flavour.

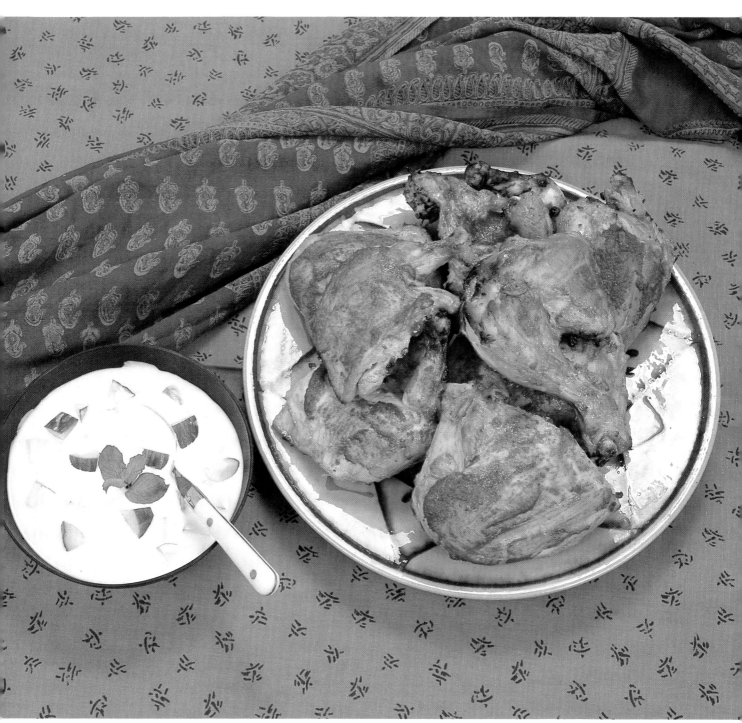

A colourful dish of tandoori chicken shown with a bowl of yoghurt and cucumber

chicken maryland

Before the Colonel from Kentucky made his reputation with chicken, this style of cooking was known as 'Maryland', which is where it originally developed, in the great farm and plantation houses of that early, rich colony. At its best it is one of the most delicious ways of eating chicken, at its worst it can be a soggy, grotty mess. The secret lies in having a properly flavoured blend of home-made breadcrumbs and sufficiently hot and deep oil to get the frying right. Don't be tempted to serve the chicken with every kind of bit and piece in sight, but stick to the traditional garnish of corn fritters and flour dipped fried bananas.

Double-bladed knife
1 chicken cut up into portions – or 8 chicken drum sticks, large size
3 slices of bread
1 teaspoon each tarragon and thyme
1 egg
4 tablespoons milk
1 tablespoon mustard, American for choice, English is OK but reduce the quantity to half
oil for frying

If you are using a whole chicken bone it as much as possible, or otherwise tidy up the drum sticks. Put the bread, torn into pieces, and the herbs into the bowl and process for 10 seconds, scrape down and process again for 10 seconds until you have fine breadcrumbs. Process the eggs and the mustard together until smooth, then pour into a bowl. Coat the chicken drum sticks first with the egg and then with the breadcrumb and herb mixture. If there's enough breadcrumbs and egg give them a double coating. In a flat-bottomed frying pan that has a lid, heat 1/4 in.–1/3 in. oil until a cube of bread will brown in it in 30 seconds. Add all the chicken pieces as close together as you can – be careful of the spitting fat as you lower them in. When they have cooked for 3 minutes on each side, turn the heat down, cover with the lid and leave for another 10–15 minutes. This won't stop the outside from going crisp but it will cook the inside to a juicy perfection.
Take the chicken out, and before serving drain it on kitchen paper.

sweet corn fritters

4 oz (100 g) flour
1 egg
1/4 pint (150 ml) milk
1 × 111/2 oz (337 g) can sweetcorn
1/4 teaspoon salt
black pepper
oil for frying

Put the flour, salt and egg into the bowl. Turn on and with the motor running add the milk through the feed-tube. Process for a further 5 seconds before stopping the motor and adding the drained sweetcorn and a good grinding of black pepper. Process briefly (2–3 seconds) to mix.
Heat a couple of spoonfuls of oil in a frying pan and drop in a few spoonfuls of the fritter mixture. After 2 or 3 minutes turn the fritters to cook on the other side. Drain them on kitchen paper and keep warm while you cook the remaining fritters.
When you have finished you can add some butter to the remaining oil and fry the flour coated bananas.

cutlets milanese

With the price of veal gone through the roof, a nice alternative to the classic Italian crispy fired fillets of veal called *Milanese*, is to do a similar thing with tender lamb chops. The combination of juicy lamb and crisp coating is delicious, eat it either with fresh vegetables or with plainly boiled new potatoes and a garlic flavoured mayonnaise, made in the processor of course.

Double-bladed knife
Grating disc
8 lamb chops, chined (the top bone removed and any
    excessive fat removed)
1 egg
2 slices of bread
4 oz (100 g) hard, dry cheese (Parmesan is best, Cheddar is
    OK)
1 teaspoon oregano
oil for frying

Grate the cheese into the bowl. Replace the grating disc with the double-bladed knife and add the bread, torn into pieces and the oregano, and process until very fine bread-crumbs. Beat the egg, then dip each chop first into the egg, then into the breadcrumbs, repeating the process twice if you have enough egg and breadcrumbs left. The crafty way to do this is to use one hand for the wet side, i.e. the egg dipping and one hand for the dry side with the bread-crumbs. When the chops are completely coated, leave them to set, preferably in the fridge, and for at least 10 minutes. Heat 1/4 in. of oil in a deep, flat-bottomed frying pan until it's hot but not smoking. When you are ready to eat add the chops to the hot oil. Fry quickly for two to four minutes on each side and drain them on quilted paper before serving them as suggested above.

shrimps thermidor

Originally this dish was made with lobster, and if you suddenly inherit a fortune, or win the pools, you could still use lobster, but large frozen shrimps make a realistic and scrumptious substitute. The dish is called *Thermidor* after the name the French revolutionaries gave the month of August in their calendar. Thermidor was supposed to be a hot month and the sauce for this dish likewise; hot with mustard, not chili. Served with rice this makes a very special dinner party meal indeed. You can also serve it in much smaller quantities, as a rather grand first course.

Double-bladed knife
1 lb (450 g) frozen shelled shrimps (the larger each
    individual fish the better)
1/4 pint (150 ml) milk
1/4 pint (150 ml) apple juice
1 oz (25 g) flour
1 1/2 (40 g) butter
4 tablespoons double cream
1 level dessertspoon mustard powder
1/2 teaspoon sugar
salt and pepper

Put all the ingredients except the flour, shrimps and cream, into a small saucepan. Heat until warm but not boiling. Pour into the bowl, switch on and add the flour in a smooth stream through the feed-tube. Process for 5 seconds until smooth. Pour back into the saucepan, put over a gentle heat and stir until the sauce thickens which it will do quite suddenly. Add the cream, turn the heat down, and simmer for 3 or 4 minutes. When you're ready to serve, add the shrimps, stir until thoroughly coated and heat for not more than 2 minutes, otherwise the shrimps tend to go rubbery. Serve it poured into a baking dish sprinkled with just a little grated Parmesan, Gruyère or Cheddar cheese. Brown briskly under the grill for not more than 1 minute. Serve on a bed of rice.

saté

Eating pieces of meat grilled on skewers is a habit that exists across the world. Called *brochettes* in France, *kebabs* in the Middle East and *saté* in the Far East. They have the same basic principle, but the Eastern pieces of meat tend to be smaller and the sauces more exciting. They are also often very hard work, grinding up the ingredients in a pestle and mortar, however, with a processor the days of almost instant *saté* sauces are upon us. And it's a flavour you shouldn't miss. It's equally at home cooked on a barbecue or under the grill. The important thing is to keep the pieces of meat quite small and to serve each guest lots of little skewers rather than one or two great big thumping ones. Although this recipe calls for lamb; chicken or beef are equally good and provide a different variety of tastes and textures.

1 lb (450 g) boneless lamb
6 tablespoons soy sauce
1 tablespoon brown sugar
1 small onion
1 clove garlic
1/2 teaspoon chili powder
4 oz (100 g) roasted peanuts
1 cup water
1 tablespoon lemon juice

Cut the meat into small neat slices about 1 in. × 1/2 in. × 1/4 in. Put these to marinate in a 4 tablespoons of the soy sauce mixed with the brown sugar and the lemon juice. Put the roasted peanuts into the bowl, add the remaining two tablespoons of soy sauce, the peeled and quartered onion and clove of garlic. Process for 10 seconds, scrape down the sides, and process again for another 10 seconds until the peanuts are really finely ground and mixed with the other ingredients. When ready to cook, thread 3 or 4 pieces of meat onto each small skewer – you can buy or even make fine bamboo skewers, about 9 in. long, but metal skewers are OK. Spread the meat out so that it is as flat as possible for quick grilling. Empty the peanuts into a saucepan, add the remaining marinade and a cup of water and heat through until boiling. Do not despair if it looks dreadful at first. The sauce will suddenly thicken and go creamy and shiny. Add the chili powder and test for seasoning at this stage. Grill the meat on a high heat for about 3 minutes each side; a barbecue, or an ordinary domestic grill is fine. To serve, pour a little of the creamy peanut sauce over the sticks and serve a bowl of it separately as well. Rice is the perfect accompaniment and a crisp salad perhaps one with a little fruit, like pineapple or apple. If you have any of the sauce left use it for sandwiches or on toast, it makes ordinary peanut butter pale into insignificance.

The crafty cook barbecues for the whole family. The picture opposite shows the saté being cooked on little wooden skewers

suprême of braised beef

In Britain, the cut we know as topside is very often used as a roast. The French however, have another way of dealing with it which makes this rather dry piece of meat so succulent that I don't think you'll ever simply roast it again. You'll need an oval shaped casserole for the job, either in metal or earthenware, but it must not be too large and the meat should fit in without too much room to rattle around. It's the kind of meal to serve for a really special Sunday lunch, and despite the special flavours it's really so easy to prepare that it could become a regular occurence in your house. One of the potato dishes from central France like *pommes dauphinoise* on page 85 goes marvellously with this.

Double-bladed knife
3–3½ lb (1.5 kg) piece of topside
4 oz (100 g) mushrooms
½ lb (225 g) onions
8 oz (225 g) carrots
3 stalks celery
⅓ pint (200 ml) apple juice
bay leaf
1 teaspoon instant coffee (don't panic, just stay with the recipe)
½ cupful processor chopped fresh parsley
2 oz (50 g) butter
salt and pepper

Peel the carrots and onions and cut them and the celery into chunks. Wash the mushrooms in hot water. Put all the vegetables into the bowl and process for 10 seconds. Scrape the sides down and process again for 2 or 3 seconds until you have an even diced effect. Melt the butter in a small saucepan and fry the vegetables gently, for 10 minutes. If you like it, you can add a clove or two of garlic cut in quarters at this stage. Don't let it burn. This process is called making a duxelles. Leave it to cool a little.

Brown the beef in the piece, either in a large frying pan or in the casserole, if it's cast iron. You don't need fat for this just get the pan or the casserole really hot. Layer the duxelles into the base of the casserole, season and put the piece of meat on top of it, pour over it the apple juice mixed with the instant coffee – you'll have to trust me, it won't taste like instant coffee when it's finished. Season, add the bay leaf, seal tightly and cook for 1½ to 2 hours in a medium, mark 3, 325°F, 160°C oven. A little bit more time won't hurt but turn the oven down once the meat's properly cooked. It should be tender, but still carvable and not totally falling to pieces. You can cook baked potatoes or the *gratin dauphinoise* in the oven at the same time. To serve it, take the meat out and put it on a warm serving dish or carving board. Stir the parsley, the remains of the duxelles and the juices in the pan together, adding a little extra apple juice, water, or if you're feeling very rich, cream. Bring the whole lot to the boil in a small saucepan and use a little to pour over the meat and use the rest as a delicious flavoursome gravy.

Steak pizzaiolla — spooning the pepper and tomato sauce over the steaks

steak pizzaiolla

A favourite from the part of Italy east of the Appenines, (the other side from Rome), where they like their food pretty spicy and in a significantly different tradition from *spaghetti bolognese* and *pizza*. This is an unusual and piquant sauce, served here with steak, but one which goes equally well with lamb.

Double-bladed knife
Slicing disc
4 entrecôte steaks
1 large onion
2 cloves garlic
a green, and if possible a red pepper
small tin (7 oz (175 g)) Italian tomatoes
1/2 teaspoon sugar
1 teaspoon lemon juice
generous pinch chili powder
1 teaspoon oregano
oil for frying

Put the peeled, quartered onion; peeled garlic cloves; contents of the tin of tomatoes; herbs, spices and seasonings into the bowl and process for 5 seconds, scrape down the bowl and process again for another 10 seconds until finely blended. Take out and reserve. Fit the slicing disc, cut the green and red peppers in half, remove the seeds, nest them together like Chinese boxes and feed through the slicing disc. In a large frying pan heat a couple of tablespoons of oil. Add the green and red pepper slices and sauté for 3 or 4 minutes. When they are soft but not cooked through, move to one side of the pan, turn the heat up and add the steaks. Sear on both sides, turn the heat down, add the tomato/onion purée, stir thoroughly and cook to the desired degree of doneness – about 5 minutes for rare, 6 for medium, 71/2 –8 for well-done. Transfer the steaks to a serving dish, turn the heat up to maximum; stir the sauce thoroughly and pour it over the steaks before serving. Don't leave out the chili powder, it's quite important to the balance of the sauce, and very, very authentic.

Steak tartare shown ready to serve with egg yolks, anchovy fillets and a garnish of parsley

marvellous mince

Perhaps of all the tasks that processors make easy, mincing meat is both the most obvious and yet the most surprising. We are all used to buying 'mince' from the butcher, but this is usually made from scrag ends of pieces of beef and helps to bulk out our economy dishes and his profits. However the texture, flavour and excitement of dishes made from meat minced yourself gives one great pleasure and in the recipes that follow you'll find suggestions for lamb, as well as a number of beef recipes. What they all share is the fact that by chopping the meat yourself you're getting something that's of a totally different quality from the mince made by a butcher. The reason for this is simple; 'Butchers' mincers', for they squeeze and grind the meat together to reduce it to a finely cut consistency, while with a processor it is actually sliced. The French call it *haché*; and because it's super-sliced none of the juice or texture is squeezed out. You can have coarsely ground beef for a *chili con carné* that will be a revelation even to most Mexicans, or have lamb puréed super-fine to make the most delicious of North Indian kebabs to eat with chutneys, poppadums, and all the trimmings. And for the really adventurous, a dish where the meat never actually gets cooked, the French *steak tartare*.

One note about mincing meat that goes right the way across all these recipes: Before putting it into the bowl, cut it up in even-sized pieces, and make sure there's no bone or large chunks of gristle. The machine can cope with almost anything, but if you want smooth, evenly-minced meat you've got to start with pieces of a reasonably even size and without anything that will stop some of the bits getting cut up at the same speed as the others.

steak tartare

The very description of *steak tartare*, raw minced beef with raw egg mixed into it, eaten as it stands, it not everybody's idea of fun. But it's not a coincidence that this unusual dish, named after the central Asian nomads who were supposed to have developed it, has remained a firm favourite on gourmet menus throughout the world. You have to try it before you knock it, and once you try it you'll probably love it, as I certainly do. The taste is delicate not rough, and you can almost feel it filling you with zest and vigour. One word of warning, it's remarkably filling, so don't be tempted to serve larger portions than I suggest.

Double-bladed knife
1 lb (450 g) rump or sirloin steak
1 onion
1 gherkin
4 teaspoons chopped parsley (done in the processor)
1 level teaspoon each, grainy French mustard, lemon
    juice, Worcester sauce, oil
1 whole egg
4 egg yolks
salt
freshly ground black pepper
4 drops tabasco

Put the whole egg, all the seasonings and vegetables into the bowl and process for 10 seconds until a smooth purée. Add the meat cut into neat cubes with the fat and gristle removed and process for another 10–15 seconds until thoroughly blended, but not chopped too fine – a little texture is important here. Remove and pat into a smooth giant hamburger shape on the serving dish. When you separate the 4 eggs, keep the yolks in a half shell, and nestle the half shells around the giant hamburger shape. You can, if you like add some anchovy in a pattern between the eggs. Serve it as it stands for each diner to mix an egg yolk into his own meat. Crisp salad and a baked potato on a side plate are my favourite accompaniments. Do try it, it may make you feel a little nomadic yourself.

hamburgers

I make no apology for including this recipe for hamburgers because the texture and juiciness of the meat when minced properly makes this common or garden dish a revelation. Don't be tempted to add any other ingredients, the basic flavour of the beef comes through far better if not too heavily disguised.

Double-bladed knife
1¼ lb (550 g) chuck steak
1 small or ½ a large onion
1 egg yolk
1 teaspoon each, salt and freshly ground black pepper
oil for frying

Cut the meat into even-sized cubes, leaving on any fat but removing all gristle. Process for 10 seconds, scrape down the sides; flash the motor on and off again to make sure it's all thoroughly evenly cut, then turn into a separate bowl. Add the onion and egg yolk to the bowl and process until puréed, add to the meat with the salt and pepper. Mix all the ingredients thoroughly together, divide into 4 and shape into 1 in. thick patties with smooth, round sides. Let these stand if you can, in the fridge for a few minutes, and then barbecue them or fry them in a minimum of oil in a thick bottomed frying pan. If you like them rare, a minute on each side on high and then 5 minutes over a low flame will do it; if you like them a little bit better done, a minute on each side and 7 to 8 minutes is about right. You can eat them in buns, with the traditional gherkins, tomato sauce, mustard and relishes, or add a little lemon juice and Worcester sauce to the juices in the pan – and serve them as a meat dish with potatoes and vegetables. In the latter case they are called a variety of names, some grand and some humble, but Cambridge Steak is the one that I have heard used the most.

Preparing the hamburgers:
Place the trimmed and cubed meat in the bowl and process until finely chopped. Turn the mixture onto a board and shape into hamburgers

cauliflower lasagne

This is a personal adaptation of one of Italy's most famous pasta dishes. It incorporates one of the old British favourites, 'cauliflower cheese', in what I think you will find is an extremely unusual way. It's also a very cheap and yet quite grand way of feeding quite a lot of people.

Grating disc
Double-bladed knife
1 large cauliflower
8 oz (225 g) Italian lasagne (flat pasta, approximately 9 in. long, 2 in. wide)
1 lb (450 g) stewing steak
1 tablespoon oil
1 onion
1 teaspoon garlic salt
1 tin Italian tomatoes
1 teaspoon each, basil and oregano
8 oz (225 g) cheese (Gouda or cheddar)
1 pint (600 ml) milk
2 tablespoons each, butter and flour
salt and pepper

Grate the cheese and set aside. Cut the stewing steak into evenly sized 1 in. cubes. Place in the bowl with the double-bladed knife and process for approximately 10 seconds until chopped medium fine. Put this into a heated frying pan with a tablespoon of oil and fry swiftly until brown. Quarter the onion and add with the contents of the tin of tomatoes to the bowl. Process until chopped, add to the meat mixture with the garlic salt, herbs and seasonings and simmer for 15 minutes. Rinse out the bowl and then use the milk, flour, butter and seasonings to make a *bechamel* sauce (see page 40). Add half the cheese, stir until smooth and set aside. Clean the cauliflower and break into small 1 in.–2 in. florets. Use these to cover the bottom of a large buttered baking dish and pour over a third of the cheese sauce, spreading it so that they are all a little covered. Fill a pudding basin with very hot water and dip the sheets of pasta into this so that they are thoroughly wet; they will probably go a little soft. Cover the cauliflower with a layer of pasta, add half the meat and tomato mixture, another third of the cheese sauce and another layer of pasta. Then the rest of the meat sauce, another layer of pasta and the remaining third of the cheese sauce on top. Sprinkle with the reserved cheese and bake the whole dish in an oven at gas mark 4, 350°F, 175°C for an hour. It will keep for an extra half hour if you turn down the temperature of the oven after it has cooked for 40 to 45 minutes. Therefore it is a very good dish to serve guests whose arrival-time you are not certain about. It will feed at least 6 people generously.

lamb kebabs

This is from the Middle East though variations of this dish are to be found from Morocco to Afghanistan. They all have slightly different flavours and textures but they are very hard work to make. That is of course until processors get to the Middle East – because with your handy helper in the kitchen you are no more than a minute away from what can take an hour and a half in the foothills of the Himalayas.

Either way these unusual minced kebabs are delicious served either as an Eastern sandwich inside some of that Greek pitta-type bread, an Indian chappati or as a main dish on a plate with rice or fried potatoes, which are so dear to the Turks' hearts. It's one of the original meals on a stick this. Don't be afraid to experiment with other flavourings and herbs if you fancy a bit more of a culinary cook's tour.

Double-bladed knife
1 lb (450 g) boneless lean lamb or mutton
1 tablespoon rice flour (or ground rice)
1 tablespoon lemon juice
1 teaspoon Worcester sauce
1 teaspoon curry powder
1 teaspoon garlic salt
1 peeled onion
salt and pepper

Cut the lamb into cubes, add it with all the other ingredients to the bowl. Process for 20 seconds, scrape down the sides and process again until the mixture is really smooth. This is traditionally done in a pestle and mortar and takes at least an hour to get the really smooth consistency needed. When finished, shape into rolls, about 4 in.–5 in. long and 1 in. thick and put these, if there is time, in the fridge to chill for 1/4 hour, then thread each one separately on to a skewer. Grill under a preheated grill or barbecue for 5 minutes each side.

chili con carné

This is almost regarded as the national dish of Mexico, although its real origins come from rather further north, and it has at least as much Texas as Mexico in its parentage. Nevertheless, it's another of those marvellous exotic and economical dishes which can be served either as a family supper, or for a grander occasion for friends and relations. It's best served with rice, to which you've added for the last 5 minutes of cooking, a packet of frozen sweetcorn (thus saving on washing-up as well). In California, where Mexican food is a new-found fashion, they sometimes serve it with a separate bowl of sour cream which is unusual, but like so many things Californian, quite nice when you try it.

It is important in this recipe not to over-mince the meat, because a certain 'bitey' texture is quite important to the finished dish.

Double-bladed knife
1 lb (450 g) chuck steak
2 tablespoons oil
8 oz (225 g) onions
1 teaspoon each, cinnamon, ground cumin, paprika and
    pinch of cayenne pepper
or 1-2 teaspoons chili powder
1 × 16 oz (450 g) tin tomatoes
1 × 16 oz (450 g) tin red kidney beans (baked-beans won't
    do for this one)
salt and pepper

Cut the meat into 1 in.–1½ in. cubes and process lightly for 2 or 3 seconds, until the meat is minced but still in discernible pieces; (this is really a stew, not a kind of soup.) Fry the mince in a big pan in a couple of tablespoons of oil until it's well browned. Add the onions to the bowl and chop finely, before adding the tin of tomatoes through the feed-tube with the motor running. Stir the spices into the meat, and season with salt and pepper. You can add a teaspoon of oregano at this stage, (it's very much an optional extra, even in Mexico). Add the tomato and onion mixture then bring to the boil before adding the contents of the tin of beans. Turn the heat down to low; cover and simmer gently for at least half an hour. The longer this dish cooks the better it tastes, and an hour is ideal. It will turn a dark rich red and the beans will absorb the flavour of both the meat and the herbs.

italian meatballs

This is on the surface an Italian recipe, but really it comes from New York. Some of the best aspects of Italian cooking came over with the immigrants of the late nineteenth century who married their rustic techniques with the amazing ingredients found in the 'land of the free'. It's solid country fare for hungry people, so don't be tempted to spare the garlic.

Double-bladed knife
1 lb (450 g) chuck steak
2 slices wholemeal bread
2 onions
1 egg
4 cloves garlic
2 teaspoons Worcester sauce
1 teaspoon each, oregano, basil, thyme
1 large tin Italian tomatoes
3–4 tablespoons oil
2 tablespoons butter
1 teaspoon sugar
1 teaspoon lemon juice
1 lb (450 g) Italian spaghetti
salt and pepper

Cut the meat into small cubes and break the bread into chunks. Peel the onions and garlic cloves. Process the meat until medium-coarse (about 7–8 seconds) then add the bread, one onion, 2 cloves of garlic, the oregano and the egg and process for 5–7 seconds or until well mixed; Form into 1 in.–1½ in. meatballs and fry until lightly browned in 1 to 2 tablespoons of oil. Add the second onion and remaining garlic to the bowl, process until puréed then with the motor running add the tomatoes, the remaining herbs, the sugar, the Worcester sauce and the lemon juice and seasonings and process briefly. Melt the butter and the remaining oil in a separate saucepan; add the tomato mixture, and cook, stirring regularly for at least 10 minutes. An extra 15 minutes partially covered with a lid and on a low heat improves the flavour remarkably, as does a bay leaf if you have it to spare. Add the meatballs to the tomato sauce, partially cover the pan, and simmer for another 15 minutes while cooking the spaghetti. When cooked arrange the spaghetti in a big ring on a large plate and pour the meatball and tomato sauce mixture into the middle.

and so to veg

Cook vegetables the crafty way and you may find yourself not bothering with the meat! Some of these dishes stand up very well on their own. The first of them, Sprouts Polonaise, (crisp sprouts – buttery breadcrumbs – creamy egg), can be served as a supper dish in its own right, and the same thing goes for the Jerusalem Artichokes Provençale. On the other hand, some of the recipes are specially designed to be eaten *with* things – Carrots Vichy, the classic French way of preparing carrots, or Spinach á la Crème – make superb accompaniments to properly roasted beef, or the Lamb Cutlets Milanese (page 67). There are also one or two unusual ideas borrowed from the Chinese and these produce really extraordinarily crisp, bright, and sharp tastes.

Sprouts polonaise, jerusalem artichokes provençale, ratatouille

sprouts polonaise

The French have a habit of identifying styles of cooking by the countries they think they first met them in and I don't know if anyone in Poland ever did use this lovely combination of butter-fried garlic flavoured breadcrumbs and crumbled hardboiled eggs, but it's a combination that I use particularly with sprouts as it brings out their nuttiness and crispness. You can serve Sprouts Polonaise as a first course, with simple grilled meats, or, as a supper dish in its own right with lots of wholemeal brown bread.

Double-bladed knife
1½ lb (675 g) sprouts
2 slices white bread
2 oz (50 g) butter
½ teaspoon garlic salt
2 hardboiled eggs
1 tablespoon lemon juice
½ teaspoon ground black pepper

Clean the sprouts carefully but do not cut the traditional cross in their base. Put them in a steamer if you have one, or if not in about 1½ in. hot water. Add a pinch of salt, bring them to the boil and cook or steam them for not more than 7 or 8 minutes. Take one out and test it! It should be cooked all the way through, bright green and still a little crisp to the bite at the heart. Drain, then cover them to keep them warm. While the sprouts are cooking, roughly break up the bread slices and process them until you have fine breadcrumbs. Melt 1½ oz (40 g) of butter in a frying pan, and stirring gently fry the crumbs until they are a golden brown. Sprinkle the garlic salt over them and keep them aside until the sprouts are ready. Shell the hardboiled eggs, cut them in half and remove the yolks. Put the whites into the bowl and process until they too are finely chopped, and keep them. With a fork break up the yolks until they also resemble breadcrumbs. You can do this in the processor with a large quantity, but 2 yolks get a little lost. When all the ingredients are ready, heat up the frying pan, add another ½ oz (12 g) of butter and the lemon juice and sizzle the sprouts very quickly for about ½ minute before adding the breadcrumbs and turning them both together. Turn into a warm serving dish and sprinkle over the egg white followed by a neat pattern of the crumbled yolk and black pepper over the top.

ratatouille

The classic Southern French vegetable dish which blends aubergines and courgettes, tomatoes, onions and green peppers, to make a superb ragoût. The virtue of the dish is that not only is it delicious at the time you cook it, but it can be eaten cold and even heats up to advantage. For me the wild thyme and lavender scented hills of Provence, with views over the deep blue Mediterranean, are conjured up every time I see and taste this so evocative dish.

Slicing disc
Double-bladed knife
½ lb (225 g) aubergines
½ lb (225 g) courgettes
½ lb (225 g) green peppers
1 red pepper
½ lb (225 g) onions
1 lb (450 g) tomatoes or 1 tin of Italian tomatoes –
    weighing 1 lb (450 g)
1 clove garlic
4 tablespoons oil
1 teaspoon each, basil and oregano
salt and pepper

Wash and clean all the vegetables, de-seeding the peppers carefully. Pack them into the feed-tube with the slicing disc in position and slice the onions, peppers, courgettes and aubergines (you may have to cut these in half to fit the feed-tube). Sprinkle the courgettes and aubergines with a little salt and leave them to drain for 20 minutes or so. Rinse the salt off and you're ready to proceed. Heat the oil in a deep frying pan, big enough to take all the vegetables, peel the clove of garlic, crush it roughly with a knife and put it in the oil to cook until light gold. Add all the vegetables, except the tomatoes, turn them in the oil and leave them to simmer for 5 minutes. If you're using a tin of tomatoes, simply open it and pour the contents into the processor fitted with the doubled-bladed knife. If you are using fresh tomatoes, just cut them in quarters before placing them in the processor. Process for about 10 seconds, until you get a coarse purée. When the vegetables in the pan have cooked for 5 minutes, season them with salt and pepper and add the tomato mixture. If it's very dry, you can add a tablespoon or two of water as it cooks, but basically the stew should cook in its own juices and in the garlic flavoured oil. Put it over a very low heat, do not cover and leave it for about 30 minutes, turning it occasionally, then sprinkle on the herbs and test for seasoning. The vegetable should still be separate and distinguishable but have blended into a delicious soft coherent whole. The dish is nice hot, cold or even re-heated.

jerusalem artichokes provençale

Jerusalem artichokes look like potatoes with knobs on. Don't let this slightly strange arrangement put you off, they have a lovely, delicious hazelnutty flavour. The real problem comes if you decide to try and peel them, avoid any recipe that requires it! Serve this as a separate course on its own or, if you feel like a light supper, a couple of fried eggs served on top is traditional and extremely delicious. You need some bread to help mop up the juice afterwards, by the way.

Slicing disc
Double-bladed knife
1 lb (450 g) Jerusalem artichokes
1 large onion
2 cloves garlic
A small tin Italian tomatoes
1 oz (25 g) butter
1 tablespoon oil
1/2 teaspoon each, sweet basil and oregano
salt and pepper

Wash the artichokes and cut off any outrageously shaped bits or pieces that are discoloured. Pack them into the feed-tube and slice them before rinsing them in a colander. Melt the oil and butter in a large, thick frying pan and when it's foaming, add the artichoke slices in an even layer, give them a little shake and turn the heat down. Meanwhile, without washing out the bowl, change the slicing disc for the double-bladed knife and add the peeled, quartered onion, the peeled garlic and the tin of tomatoes. Process for 10 seconds until a fairly smooth purée is obtained. Turn the artichokes over with a fish slice, add the onion and tomato mixture and simmer for about 30 minutes until the liquid has almost dried up, a thick jammy sauce is left, and the artichokes are soft. Sprinkle the vegetables with the herbs, salt and pepper, and serve it either in the frying pan or in a white china dish where the rich colours of the sauce are shown off best.

carrots vichy

Vichy is the part of France where the famous spa water is believed to be perfect for cooking carrots. Only the French, I think, would go to the trouble of working out the right water, but the right technique they certainly do have. This produces lovely buttery, slightly candied carrots which are an absolute pleasure. Make sure you make twice as many as you think you need for that's how many people will eat.

Slicing disc
2 lb (900 g) carrots
1 1/2 oz (40 g) butter
1 tablespoon sugar
pinch of salt

Peel the carrots, *pack* them vertically into the feed-tube and slice them a batch at a time. Melt the butter in a wide saucepan and having turned the carrot slices in it quickly, add a pinch of salt, enough water to *barely* cover them, and finish by sprinkling the sugar on. Bring to the boil and cook them for about 12 minutes. They are ready when all the water has been absorbed and a gentle sizzle is heard from the carrots just starting to fry in the butter. They may need a little more salt at this stage but they should be eaten while they are really piping hot.

mixed fried vegetables

This dish has three special advantages. One is that it's very simple to do, especially using the slicing disc, secondly it looks really pretty and thirdly it can be ready just five minutes after you've started. A great boon for unexpected guests or a quick snack before going out. Once again it uses the basic Chinese technique of stir-frying. The combination of vegetables is both pretty and unexpected, so it's a pity to use it only when you're having fried rice.

Slicing disc
Grating disc
2 green peppers
2 carrots
1 onion
1/2 lb (225 g) bean sprouts or 1/2 lb (225 g) cabbage
    shredded in the processor
2 tablespoons oil
salt and pepper

Halve and de-seed the green peppers. Peel and cut the onion in half, and peel the carrots. Put the green peppers, packed tightly together into the feed-tube and slice them and then the onion. If you're using the cabbage and not the bean sprouts, slice this too at the same time. Change the slicing disc for the grating disc and pack the carrots into the feed-tube *lengthwise* then switch on and grate them into the mixture. The lengthwise position will produce long, thin slivers of carrot. Heat 2 tablespoons of oil in a deep frying pan and add all the vegetables. Toss them swiftly for about a minute, cover for one minute more over a low heat, raise the heat again and toss once more, having seasoned generously with salt and pepper. You can add a teaspoon each of lemon juice and sugar, or a tablespoon of soy sauce and a teaspoon of butter at this stage. Both are delicious but I quite like the mixture on its own with the clear, clean taste of the vegetables brought out by the high speed cooking and the simple seasoning.

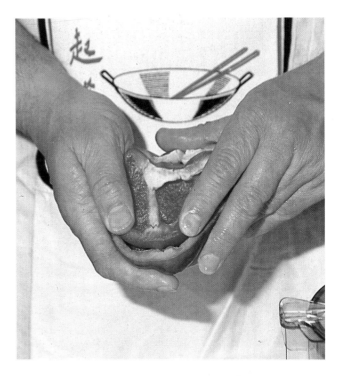

Pack the halved and deseeded peppers inside one another before putting them into the feed-tube for slicing

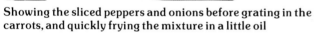

Showing the sliced peppers and onions before grating in the carrots, and quickly frying the mixture in a little oil

chili ginger cabbage

Chinese cabbage is a vegetable that has recently become widely available in Britain. It looks like a very light green Cos lettuce and can be eaten either as a salad, see page 50, or cooked very quickly using the stir-fry method. The flavourings come from Szechwan, in the Western end of China, and have a rather unusual bite to them with no sign of soya sauce around.

Slicing disc
1 lb (450 g) Chinese cabbage
1 onion
1 in. long piece of fresh ginger
1/2 teaspoon chili powder
1 oz (25 g) butter
1 dessertspoon brown sugar
1/2 cup water
3 tablespoons oil
salt

Take off any discoloured leaves from the cabbage and cut it lengthwise into quarters. Press it in the feed-tube with the slicing disc in position and slice it quarter by quarter. Put aside and then slice the onion. Peel the ginger root, chop it finely. Heat the oil in a large frying pan, add the ginger and let it sizzle for about 30 seconds, then add the onions and turn them, and then the cabbage pieces. Turn them rapidly for about a minute and half making sure they all get coated with the ginger flavoured oil, and are heated through thoroughly. Add the butter, the brown sugar, the water and a good teaspoon of salt. Cook over a very high heat for another minute to minute and a half. Cover and leave for one minute more, remove the cover – turn the heat back up to high, sprinkle on the chili powder, toss rapidly for another 30 seconds, and serve in a heated bowl with all the juices poured over it. If you don't like your food too spicy leave out nearly all the chili.

potato galette

This is a kind of potato pie, with a crispy brown exterior and with the potatoes making their own creamy buttery filling. It can be cooked in a pan on the top of a stove, or, if you like, in the oven. Either way the key to the whole dish is the super thin slicing that the processor does so effortlessly, and the careful washing of the potatoes before you cook them.

Slicing disc
2 lb (900 g) potatoes (preferably the waxy kind)
2 oz (50 g) butter
2 oz (50 g) cooking oil
salt
freshly ground black pepper
sliver of garlic

Wash and peel the potatoes, trim them to fit the feed-tube and slice them into the bowl. Empty the potato slices into a pan of clean cold water and swish them around until all the starch has been washed off and the water is quite cloudy. Take them out and drain them. Heat a frying pan or a flat oven-proof dish and put 2/3 of the oil and butter into it, let it sizzle and quickly, before it burns (having taken it off the heat) layer the potato slices around it in an even pattern building it up so that it forms a thick potato pancake. Press it down with a spatula – not your hand because steam will come sizzling out, and either turn the heat on the stove down, or place the dish in the oven to bake. Do not cover it either way. 15 minutes later put a clean serving plate over the pan and, working very carefully, invert the dish over the plate and you'll find that the galette falls out of the pan and has a brown crusty coherent bottom. Put the rest of the oil and butter into the pan to melt and swirl the sliver of garlic round in the pan. With the cooked side uppermost carefully slide the potato pancake back into the pan and either continue to fry over a low heat or put it back in the oven. 20 minutes later it's ready, with both sides crisply brown, but with the centre creamy and delicious, with a flavour of the butter and garlic. Salt and pepper at this stage, and serve it cut in wedges rather like a cake.

Potato galette

pommes dauphinoise

Just to prove they haven't run out of ideas with the sliced potatoes the French have another dish using the same basic ingredients but tasting completely different. It comes, this, from the eastern edge of France where the weather can get pretty nippy in the winter. It's a lovely warming, filling dish and incredibly rich. If you happen to have any dieters about don't serve it because it can break down the most resolute of resolves. It has another advantage, not common in potato dishes, in that it won't spoil if kept waiting and will happily sit in the oven quietly for an extra half hour or so without coming to any harm.

Slicing disc
1½ lb (675 g) waxy potatoes
1 clove garlic
2 oz (50 g) butter
½ pint (300 ml) creamy milk
salt and pepper

Peel the potatoes and slice them finely using the slicing disc and then rinse them in a bowl of clean cold water until all the starch is washed off. Take a deep earthenware casserole and rub it carefully with a cut clove of garlic (you can add more if you like.) Smear the inside of the dish with a little of the butter and then layer the potatoes into it, until you have used them all up. Every inch or so dot in some knobs of butter and sprinkle salt and pepper over them. Pour in the milk, add another few dots of butter and some salt and pepper to the top, cover and put in a mark 4, 350°F, 175°C oven to bake for 1 hour. Take the lid off and leave for another 20 minutes for it to form a crisp crust. At this stage you can turn the oven down, cover the dish and leave it for up to another 45 minutes without it coming to any harm. The garlic, butter and milk combine with the potatoes to form an incredibly delicious coherent mass halfway towards mashed potatoes but with enough texture to compliment the delicate and unexpectedly rich flavour. Traditionally this is served with roast lamb, and I must say, I don't think I've ever found a better partner for it.

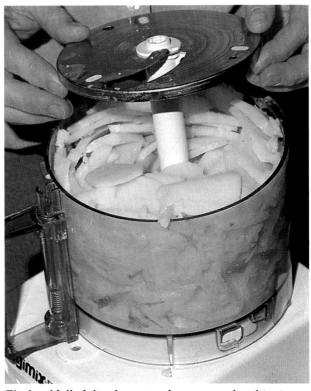

The bowl full of sliced potatoes for pommes dauphinoise

Washing off the starch in a bowl of cold water

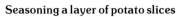

Seasoning a layer of potato slices

Pouring on the milk just before baking

The pommes dauphinoise browned in the oven and ready to serve

purées

sprout purée

That otherwise much under-rated vegetable the brussels-sprout is almost uneatable later on in the season when it becomes loose and a bit floppy. This recipe comes to the rescue, in fact it's so delicious, that I even make it when I can buy the hard, crisp, nutty sprouts left by the early frosts of winter. Once again incredibly hard work without a processor but merely a whisk away, with your friendly kitchen aid. Don't stint on the butter or black pepper in this recipe, they really do make a colossal difference.

Double-bladed knife
1½ lb (675 g) brussels-sprouts
2 oz (50 g) butter
1 dessertspoon of freshly ground black pepper
1 tablespoon of lemon juice
salt

Clean the sprouts, not discarding any part except the discoloured leaves. Put them in a pan of boiling water and cook for about 7 minutes, leaving them still bright green but cooked through. Drain thoroughly and process them for 10 seconds, then stop, scrape down the sides and process again until a fairly smooth purée is achieved. Add the butter, lemon juice, a good pinch of salt and the black pepper, process again until thoroughly mixed. Pile into a white china serving bowl. It's absolutely delicious as an accompaniment to almost all roast meat dishes.

spinach à la crème

Back to France for this dish, where I'm afraid, as is only too often the case, they know how to make the best of the vegetables that we grow so well. If spinach has always made you feel that it was best left to Popeye, I do urge you to try this dish, just once. It could change your life because the combination of flavour and texture, is something that only specialist chefs can normally achieve. I'm extremely fond of this dish eaten on its own, with triangles of bread fried in butter, the crispness of the butter fried-bread and the creamy delicate green of the spinach is sensational, but it's also quite a grand vegetable to go with one of your special fish or chicken dishes. Do take the trouble to buy fresh spinach, frozen spinach can be cooked like this, but just doesn't have the same strength of flavour, or vibrant colour.

Double-bladed knife
2 lb (900 g) spinach
3 fl oz (90 ml) small carton double cream
2 oz (50 g) butter
black pepper
salt

Wash the spinach carefully and trim off any thick stalks. Place it in a large saucepan without any water except that which is left on it from the washing. Cover it with a lid and put it over a high heat, for about 3 minutes. Take off the lid, stir and cook it with the lid off until it dries out, surprisingly spinach cooked like this will produce more liquid than you would believe. The process should take about 5 minutes. When the liquid is almost dried out of the spinach pan add the butter and toss the spinach and butter together until the butter has melted and the spinach is properly coated. Put the cream into a separate pan, and heat it gently. Put the spinach into the bowl and process for 5 seconds, scrape down the sides, process again for another 5 seconds and with the motor running pour in the very hot (just below boiling point) cream. Do not be tempted to use more than a 3 fl oz carton as otherwise the vegetable will become too runny. Season with salt and black pepper. I'm quite fond of a little grate of nutmeg with this dish as well, for it seems to bring out the flavour of the spinach and butter particularly nicely.

Ingredients for spinach à la crème

punchep

This is really a rustic vegetable dish from my Welsh childhood, but with a processor it is turned into something more delicate. If you like your food a touch rustic process for a little bit less time than I recommend and you'll get the grainy texture that I remember so well from my youth.

Double-bladed knife
1 lb (450 g) carrots
1 lb (450 g) yellow swedes
2 oz (50 g) butter
black pepper
salt

Peel the carrots and swedes and cut them into large dice, about an inch across. Boil them in lightly salted water for about 15 minutes until they are thoroughly cooked, but not falling apart. Drain them and leave them to stand in the colander, for about 3 minutes, to remove any surplus liquid. Place them in the bowl and process for 10 seconds. Add the butter, scrape down the sides, season with salt and plenty of black pepper and process again until the mixture is smooth and fluffy.

pastry makes perfect

Pastry is always a delicate subject and in more than one way. Most people who cook have their own methods and opinions on pastry, with some, it's a packet mix, and with others it's a skilled process they have learnt at their mother's knee. For many people, it's a horror story; never able to get pastry right, to have it work, roll out or do any of the other things that their friends seem to find effortless.

The key to pastry is the amount you handle it. The less, the better, because coolness and speed, whatever the method are essential. This is where a processor comes in, it rubs in and mixes, not in a twinkling of an eye, but in not very much longer and, of course, as it's untouched by human hands the pastry stays cool, calm and controllable in a way that only the very best pastry chefs can achieve. Having said all that, there are still a few chasms to cross such as, 'What sort of pastry?' The French and the English have very different views on the matter. The English like it soft and flaky and the French crisp and crumbly. Is the pastry meant to be something to enjoy in itself, or just a container for the goodies that you choose to put in it?

Then there's the question of to roll or not to roll. I'm an anti-roller myself, having learnt some years ago that I could often achieve just as attractive and delicious results without the business of having to balance thin, sheets of pastry over trembling rolling pins. But of course, that's merely a way of saying it's a skill I haven't really acquired. I have suggested four different kinds of pastry in this chapter for different sorts of things. For the French open tarts called quiches, full of highly flavoured ingredients in a delicate creamy sauce; I suggest the crisp French brisée pastry. For the rather more solid recipes

from the English counties like game pie or apple pie, I use a more traditional English shortcrust. But one of my favourite things of all in the shape of pies and pastries are those delicious crisp biscuity shells filled with fresh summer fruits – strawberries, raspberries, cherries, coated in just a little gleaming glaze and looking almost too attractive to eat. To make those you need the French sablée, called sablée because it means 'sandy', which is the texture of the pastry when you bite it. Lastly, for the truly adventurous, choux pastry, the stuff that eclairs are made of and cooks reputations shattered by, unless you happen to have a processor in your kitchen. With all these pastries, the amazing processor makes many of the most skilled and difficult parts of the work effortless, and also speeds up the whole process quite remarkably.

As someone who's not a natural pastry maker, one of the secrets I've discovered over the years is that a degree of confidence is very important. Get all the ingredients together, make sure you know what to do before you start, and then *do* it. Flat out, and without losing your nerve half way. It's amazing what a difference that particular style makes to any pastry making. Indeed, it's not a bad rule for cooking in general.

Don't skip the thirty minutes in the fridge that I recommend for all the pastries. It makes sure that they hardly shrink when they are cooked, and it also makes them a great deal easier to handle when you are rolling or pressing out into the tins or dishes. Don't forget either, the occasional decoration with scraps. A little bit of pastry rolled out flat, cut in the shape of a leaf or two, and stuck on with a drop of water or egg makes such an attractive decoration.

This onion quiche *(see page 95)* **is equally good if eaten hot, warm or cold**

pâte brisée
French Savoury Pastry

Pâte brisée is the French answer to savoury pastry. It's traditionally made as a container for the mixtures that make the huge variety of quiches and open pies that the French adore as first courses, or as a main course for a light meal. It's rather a tougher material than our shortcrust pastry and can be handled more firmly and shaped more thinly. The key to this extra strength is the egg yolk which goes into the pastry. Don't be tempted to leave it out. The quantities given are for one 8–10 in. open flan.

Double-bladed knife
5 oz (150 g) flour
2 oz (50 g) butter
1 egg yolk
1/2 teaspoon salt
11/2–2 tablespoons cold water

Put the flour, salt and roughly chopped butter into the bowl and process until you have very coarse breadcrumbs (about 5 seconds). Add the egg yolk and water and process until the mixture starts to ball up around the knife. Switch off and empty the pastry onto a floured board. Gather it all together and knead it two or three times with the heel of your hand so it forms a solid coherent mass, wrap it in foil or cling film and put it in the fridge. It should be left there for at least 30 minutes, up to a couple of hours won't hurt. When you're ready to use it, you can either roll it out on a floured board in the normal manner or press it into the tin with the knuckles of your hand which is my favourite method. Put it into a hot oven, mark 6, 400°F, 200°C, whether you're baking it empty (blind) or with a filling. If you're baking it empty without a filling, make sure you've put in a piece of foil weighed down with some beans or rice to stop the pastry base puffing up in the sudden strong heat. If empty it should be baked for about 10 minutes.

To make pâte brisée process together the flour and the butter until the mixture resembles coarse breadcrumbs

Process again until the mixture forms into a ball

Stop the machine before adding the water and the egg yolk

Knead the pastry briefly before placing it in the fridge to rest

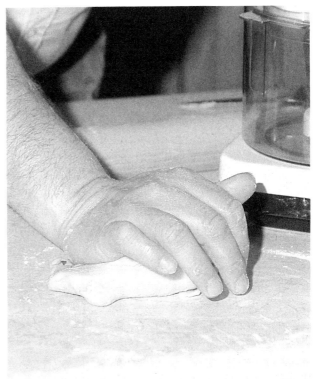

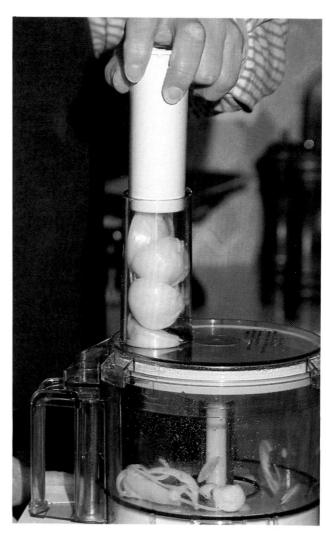

onion quiche

This is a recipe for one of the simplest of all quiches. It is both creamy and flavourful, and although there are a lot of onions, it hasn't got the kind of afterglow that makes you 'not nice-to-know'. It has the other advantage of being made with the sort of ingredients you usually have in the house. It is important to cook the onions before putting them into the *quiche*, and you can add a clove of garlic, also sliced very finely if you like.

Slicing disc
Double-bladed knife
1 lb (450 g) onions
1 tablespoon butter
2 eggs
1 egg yolk
7 fl oz (225 ml) milk
grated nutmeg
salt and pepper
1 recipe Pâte Brisée

Peel the onions and slice them finely through the slicing disc. Turn them gently in the butter for about 5 minutes until they are soft but not brown. Line a 8–9 in. flan dish with the pastry and spread the onion mixture onto that. Change to the double-bladed knife and process the eggs, egg yolk, milk and seasonings together. Pour the egg mixture gently into the flan, it should come to not more than ½ in. from the top as it will rise and overflow otherwise. Bake at mark 7, 425°F, 225°C oven for 25 minutes, turn down to mark 5, 375°F, 190°C for another 5–10 minutes until the top is well-browned and the pastry cooked through. Serve this hot or cold, but remember it will sink a little as it cools.

The photographs show the greased flan dish being dusted with flour before lining it with pastry. The slicing and cooking of the onions which are then spread over the flan. Finally the processed egg mixture is poured over and the whole dish is baked for about half an hour

cheese quiche

Despite the name *Lorraine*, the most popular quiche in France is almost certainly the one made from Gruyère cheese. It's that very rich cheese made in France, Switzerland (and probably nowadays in Ireland and Italy as well), which adds a distinctive flavour to French cooking. You can use very mature Cheddar or Leicestershire cheese, but whatever else you do, don't use any of the processed types of cheese as they simply won't blend in when they're cooked. *Cheese Quiche* is also one of those dishes that you can add your own bits to, a few mushrooms, a few spears of asparagus, some left-over cooked mixed vegetables all can be added with advantage and quite a lot of impunity on condition you don't overdo it.

Grating disc
Double-bladed knife
1 recipe Pâte Brisée
8 oz (225 g) Gruyère (or Leicester or Cheddar) cheese
2 eggs
1 egg yolk
7 fl oz (220 ml) milk
1 dessertspoon cornflour
salt and pepper

Line an 8–9 in. flan tin with pastry. Grate the cheese, take it out of the bowl, put in the double-bladed knife, add the cornflour, milk, eggs and seasonings, and process until smooth. Mix half the cheese into this mixture, and pour it into the pastry case. Season and sprinkle the rest of the cheese over the egg mixture. Make sure the total does not come to more than half an inch from the top otherwise as the pie cooks, the mixture, which rises quite a lot, will spill over the sides. Bake it at mark 7, 425°F, 225°C for 25–30 minutes. It's quite best eaten hot, as the risen pie sinks quite a lot as it cools.

quiche provençale

This pie is really a bit of a crafty cheat because the pastry is cooked in advance and the filling is really poured in and just heated up in the pastry rather than cooked with the raw shell. It's very delicious however, and again is one of those adaptable recipes that can bend to the availability of ingredients. One thing, do not be tempted to use any of those bottled pimento salads, because the vinegar and extra salt in the preserving liquid will make the pastry soggy.

Slicing disc
1 recipe Pâte Brisée
1 recipe Ratatouille (page 80)
1 oz (25 g) black olives
1 teaspoon each Basil and Oregano

Line an 8 in. flan tin with the pastry, then line it with a piece of foil and weigh it down with a handful of rice or dried beans. Bake it at mark 6, 400°F, 200°C for 10 minutes. Take the foil and beans out, bake for further 5 minutes, then leave it to cool. You can use either left-over *ratatouille* or make it fresh. Either way, fill the pie shell with warm, but not hot, *ratatouille*. Place the olives in an attractive, decorative pattern across the top, sprinkle with the mixed herbs and salt and pepper if the vegetables are not already highly seasoned. Put back in the oven for not more than 10–15 minutes, until the vegetable mixture is heated right through. When you're putting the *ratatouille* in it's a good trick to do so with a slotted spoon to drain off any extra juice that may be in the mixture.

shortcrust pastry

British Savoury Pastry

If *you* have a favourite shortcrust pastry recipe, try making it in the processor, rubbing the flour and fat in together first and adding the liquid afterwards. My own experience in this is that any recipe I'm used to making by hand probably needs a little more flour added to it when using a processor as the blending and mixing is rather more thorough than you can achieve by hand. Don't add much water, but add it bit by bit as the pastry will suddenly ball up around the knife. If you haven't got a favourite shortcrust recipe try using this one:

Double-bladed knife
6 oz (175 g) plain flour
2 oz (50 g) butter
2–3 tablespoons water
pinch salt

Put the butter, cut into two or three chunks, into the bowl with the flour and salt. Process until you have fairly coarse breadcrumbs. This takes about 5–10 seconds (you may need to scrape the sides of the bowl down once during the process). Then, with the motor running, add the water, a tablespoonful at a time. Flours vary with the amount of water they can absorb, so you'll have to check as you go. When the pastry is made, it will suddenly form a coherent ball around the knife and at this point you switch off. Scrape out the bowl thoroughly, and very gently press all the pastry pieces together into one solid lump. Wrap it in foil or cling film, put it in the fridge for about half an hour.

game pie

Traditionally, game pies were made with a kind of pastry called hot water pastry, and decorated with extravagant shapes. The traditional Grosvenor Pie is probably the last remnant of this pattern of cooking. I think that a delicious game pie can be made using shortcrust pastry and the one or two cheaper forms of game that are still available. This pie is intended to be served hot, but if you want to serve it cold, proceed as below but make it in a loaf tin rather than an oval pie dish. This will make slicing easier, and before it cools use a funnel to pour some melted jellied consommé, in through the slits in the top until it fills the pie up completely. It feeds 6 easily.

Double-bladed knife
1 recipe shortcrust pastry
2 lb (900 g) game (either back legs and saddle of a hare, or
      4 or 5 pigeons or stewing venison)
8 oz (225 g) onions
2 tablespoons dripping or oil
2 tablespoons flour
4 oz (100 g) button mushrooms
4 tablespoons redcurrant jelly
2 bay leaves
1/2 teaspoon dried thyme
1/2 teaspoon dried marjoram

Put the cleaned game in a saucepan and cover with water. Make sure there's at least an inch over the top. Bring to the boil, skim off any scum and simmer for 30 minutes. Remove the stalks from the mushrooms and add them with the peeled and quartered onions to the processor. Process until finely chopped, and then fry in the dripping or oil for 5 or 6 minutes. Sprinkle with the flour and stir until smooth. Add 3 cups of the stock in which the game was cooked and make a smooth sauce. Remove the meat from the bones of the game, cut into neat chunks and add to the sauce with the redcurrant jelly and the herbs and season generously. Line a deep (1 1/2 in.) pie dish with half the pastry, put in the game mixture, put the button mushroom caps along the top and cover with the remaining pastry rolled out thinly. Trim the edges, brush the pie with egg beaten up with a little milk, and make two deep slits in the centre for the steam to escape. Bake it in a medium oven mark 5, 375°F, 190°C for 45 minutes covering the lid with a little foil if it starts to brown before the rest of the pie is cooked.

chicken pie

A lovely farmhousy recipe, made, if you can get one, with the cheaper, and slightly more flavourful boiling fowl. The stock that's left from cooking the chicken makes a wonderful basis for a soup.

Slicing disc
1 recipe shortcrust pastry
1 boiling fowl (or roasting chicken) weighing about 3 lb (1.3 kg)
8 oz (225 g) carrots
1 lb (450 g) leeks
4 oz (100 g) button mushrooms
bay leaf
large piece parsley stalk
2 hard-boiled eggs
1 tablespoon cornflour
1 tablespoon chopped parsley

Put the chicken and the washed giblets into a saucepan big enough to hold them comfortably. Pour over water to come at least 2 in. above the chicken, bring to the boil and skim off any scum. Meanwhile, peel the carrots and clean the leeks thoroughly in running water, stripping any discoloured outer leaves. Slice the carrots and the leeks through the slicing disc and add them to the skimmed chicken pot. Add the bay leaves and parsley stalk and root, if there is one, and simmer until the chicken is tender. This may be as little as 30 minutes for a roasted chicken, 1¼ hours for a boiling fowl. Keep the lid on and don't season with salt or pepper at this stage. Wash the button mushrooms thoroughly and if they're large, cut them in half, peel the hard-boiled eggs and cut them in half. When the chicken is cooked, remove it and the vegetables from the stock, skin it and take the meat off the bones. (You can put the skin and bones back into the stock to enrich it). Mix 2 ladlefuls of the stock with the cornflour and whisk thoroughly. Mix the chicken pieces and the cooked vegetables together and fill an oval pie dish almost to the brim. Season it at this stage with salt and pepper and chopped parsley and pour over the stock and cornflour. Lay the hard boiled eggs, cut side up on top and press gently so that they're barely covered by the sauce. Take a quarter of the pastry and roll it into a long thin sausage-like shape which will fit around the rim of the dish. Moisten the edge with cold water and carefully press the pastry roll on top of it. Roll out the remaining pastry so that it fits the shape of the dish, moisten the pastry on the edge of the dish with cold water again, and lay the sheet of pastry over the top of it, using the back of a fork, mark it all the way round pressing the sheet of pastry into the sausage-shape around the edge of the dish. Trim the excess off with a knife and use it to make decorations to put on the centre of the pie. Cut a hole in the middle and bake the whole dish at mark 7, 425°F, 225°C for 25 minutes until the pastry is nicely browned on top. You can if you like, glaze the pastry with a little milk or beaten egg, before putting it into the oven. This produces a lovely shiny appearance. The chicken pie can be eaten hot or cold.

The chicken pie photographs show the chicken and vegetables in the pie dish, and then the stock being poured on after the addition of the eggs. The rolled pastry is carefully placed over the dish before being trimmed round the edge. The trimmings can then be used for decoration

english apple pie

Though there is as much dispute about what makes a good English Apple Pie as there are cooks who cook it, most people seem to agree on a single crust, thinly sliced apples and not too much spicing. The only exception sometimes being a flavouring of quince, that unusual fruit which tends only to be used for jellies or jams.

Slicing disc
1 recipe sweet shortcrust pastry
1½ lb (675 g) cooking apples
6 oz (175 g) sugar
2 tablespoons quince jelly or marmalade (optional)
grated rind of a lemon
pinch of allspice

Peel, core and halve the apples and slice them through the slicing disc. Grease an 8 in. pie dish and put in the apples sprinkling them with sugar and the lemon rind as you go. If you are using it spread the quince marmalade or jelly on the top and add the pinch of allspice. Pile the apples up in the centre so that they form a peak that is at least ½ in. above the edge of the dish. This is because the apples will almost certainly sink as they cook and the pie will otherwise have a dent in the middle. Roll the pastry out, damp the edges of the plate, place the pastry on top, trim the edges off and decorate the circumference with the back of a fork. Cut a double slot in the middle and bake at mark 6, 400°F, 200°C for 35 minutes. Turn the oven down to mark 4, 350°F, 175°C and bake for a further 10 minutes, putting a little foil over the pastry if it's browning too quickly. You can serve this pie hot or cold. If you let it get cold it'll sink a little bit from it's high point in the centre. At the point where you turn the oven down, you can, if you like, sprinkle the top with a little castor sugar which produces a nice glazed, slightly crunchy appearance.

american apple pie

Another deep dish pie, this, but with a very different flavour and texture when it's cooked. It's very often eaten in America hot out of the oven, with a large dollop of vanilla ice cream, and is known as *pie-à-la-mode*. Even if you eat it cold, it's still very nice with thick cream or ice-cream ladled on top of it.

Double-bladed knife
1½ lb (675 g) eating apples (the Americans don't have cookers)
1 tablespoon cornflour
1 tablespoon lemon juice
6 oz (175 g) sugar
1 teaspoon each of ground cinnamon and cloves
1 recipe shortcrust pastry
1 oz (25 g) butter

Put the peeled cored apples cut in quarters into the bowl with the cornflour and lemon juice and process briefly until the apples are still in chunks but chopped down quite a lot, and the cornflour and lemon juice have been mixed all over them. Line a deep pie dish with half the pastry, pile in the apple mixture, seasoning it with the sugar and the mixed spices. Make sure it's piled at least an inch higher than the edge of the dish in the middle to prevent the pie sinking in the middle when it's cooked. Dot the surface of the apples with butter and cover with the second layer of pastry, wetting the rim first to make sure it will stick. Brush the top with a little milk or beaten egg if you want a glaze, cut two slots in the centre and bake at mark 6, 400°F, 200°C for 40 minutes. Turning the oven off and letting the pie cook for another 5 minutes in the switched-off oven. It's usually served hot, but is equally delicious cold, in which case it is best to let it cool all the way down in the oven.

pâte sablée

The French version of sweet pastry, called *sablée* which is the word for sand, because it is so crisp and sugary that when eaten it just crumbles away like a sand castle in front of the tide. It's not all that dry or gritty, just incredibly soft textured, but surprisingly strong and firm carrying the fruits and cream fillings that the French are so fond of. Unlike English pastry it is also very useful for filling with raw ingredients as the shell, with the egg gives the pastry a surprising degree of water resistance and strength. This pastry is so delicious that in parts of France they don't put anything in it at all, but roll it out flat, and cut it with biscuit cutters and make what are called *sablées* or buttery biscuits. Sometimes they cover them with slivered almonds before they're baked. If you have any pastry left over it's certainly worth trying this.

Double-bladed knife
4 oz (100g) flour
1½ tablespoons castor sugar
1 egg
2 oz (50 g) butter
pinch salt

Put the flour, sugar, salt and butter, cut into chunks, into the bowl and process until it resembles fine breadcrumbs. With the motor running, add the egg and stop the machine the moment it starts to form a ball. Tip it onto a floured board, press it all together with the heel of your hand, squash it flat a couple of times, kneading it lightly, and finally roll it up into a ball before wrapping it in cling film and putting it in the fridge for at least 30 minutes. After that, it's ready to be used. It won't suffer if it's kept tightly wrapped in a fridge for up to three days.

crème pâtissière

The most sumptious part of French tartes for most foreigners is the fact that just beneath the fruit and before you get to the crisp pastry, there is a layer of what tastes like vanilla flavoured cream. It's called *crème pâtissière* or *bakers cream* and although it was originally developed as a substitute for the more expensive real stuff, I often actually prefer it. It is one of the easiest things in the world to make, and transforms an ordinary tart into something else! With a processor, of course, a lot of the art is already taken care of for you, so you can earn the plaudits without having to struggle.

Double-bladed knife
3 oz (75 g) castor sugar
2 eggs
2 oz (50 g) flour
¾ pint (450 ml) milk
½ teaspoon vanilla essence

Put the eggs into the bowl, add the sugar and process until really smoothly blended together. Add the flour and process again until smoothly mixed. Bring the milk to the boil and with the motor running, pour it carefully through the feed-tube into the bowl. Let the whole mixture be processed for a further 5 seconds. Return to the saucepan, cook over a low heat for 5 minutes, stirring much of the time until the mixture thickens completely and the flour is all cooked. Add the vanilla essence then let it cool, stirring it occasionally to prevent a skin forming, it's now ready for use. It'll keep in the fridge for up to a week if it's covered, and is really one of the nicest and most sumptuous cheap luxuries I know.

french fruit tart

Slicing disc
1 recipe pâte sablé
½ recipe créme pâtissière
2 lb (900 g) fruit – pears, peaches or plums
4 tablespoons apricot jam
4 tablespoons water

Core or stone but don't peel the fruits, cut them in half and process them through the slicing disc. You'll probably need to stop and start the machine packing the tube, each time, to help to keep the slices even and tidy. Take an 8 in. flan tin, preferably one with a removable base, and knuckle the pastry out across it (having greased it if it's not non-stick), until you have a pastry shell that comes about an ⅛ in. above the tin all the way round. Fill the centre with a piece of foil and rice or beans to weigh it down, and bake it in the oven at mark 6, 400°F, 200°C for 15 minutes. Take out the foil and let it bake for another 10 minutes. When the flan is cool fill it to within ½ in. of the top with the *créme pâtissière* which should also be cool but shouldn't be chilled. Take the fruit slices (if you've been keeping them waiting, make sure that they are in a little water with some lemon juice so that they don't go brown), lay them in circles all the way round the pie so they form a pretty scalloped overlapping pattern. Melt the apricot jam and water together until thoroughly mixed and using a pastry brush or working with a spoonful at a time, spread the glaze over the fruit, return the whole lot to the oven and cook for another 15–20 minutes making sure that the pastry doesn't burn at the edges. You can serve this hot if you like, but it is far nicer cooled down, and allowed to set. If the fruit has a little burning on the top don't worry, it's the glaze caramelising and is totally authentic.

strawberry tart

One of the great joys in France in the strawberry season are the bakers shops which appear to be absolutely inundated with tiny strawberry tarts. The pastry gold and crumbly, the fruit, uncooked, piled high in the tarts with an amazing shiny glaze over that makes it look even more sumptuous and delicious. These days they cost a small fortune, but are so easy to make at home that they are one of my favourite indulgences. One of the other virtues is that although best quality fruit is ideal you can make them with strawberries running towards the end of the season, when they are far cheaper and may not have quite the perfect shape and colour.

1 recipe of pâte sablé
½ recipe créme pâtissière
1 lb (450 g) strawberries
8 oz (225 g) strawberry jam
4 tablespoons water
1 tablespoon lemon juice

Line a series of mini tart tins (these can be the really small cup cake size or rather pretty fluted mini tart tins sold in galvanised tin ware you can find most hardware shops.) Whatever you use, line as many of the tins as you have pastry. Put a little crumpled foil in each one to prevent them going out of shape when you bake them and bake in a mark 6, 400°F, 200°C oven for 7 minutes. Take out the foil and bake for another 5 minutes or so, making sure none of the pastry starts to catch or burn. Take them out and allow them to cool, remove from their tins. Into the bottom of each one, put a couple of tablespoons of *créme pâtissière* and then pile as many strawberries as it will conveniently and attractively hold. Do remember to keep a pretty strawberry for the top of the pile for each tart, as the decoration is one of the things that makes this looks so sumptuous. Melt the strawberry jam, water and lemon juice together in a saucepan and beat it until smooth, getting rid of as many of the lumps as possible. Take a tablespoonful and trickle it over the top of each tart so that it runs down to the crevices between the strawberries, and make sure that none of the strawberries are left uncovered by the glaze. Allow to set and serve them when the whole confection is nice and cool. They are not greatly improved by being chilled in the fridge, but I have been known to put a small dollop of whipped cream right on the top even though it may be a little like gilding the lily.

A mouthwatering plate of strawberry tarts

choux pastry

Why this pastry is named after cabbages in France, I've never understood. It's the stuff that eclairs and whipped cream dreams are made of. I've suggested three possible uses, because I think self-indulgence should have some limits, but if you've ever had a confection made with choux pastry you'd like to copy, this recipe will help you to do it effortlessly. Once again it's the processor that takes the hard work out of this professional pastry. This way, you wind up cool and refreshed, with all your energies available to devour the eclairs as soon as they're ready.

Double-bladed knife
2 oz (50 g) butter
8 fl oz (250 ml) water (just under 1/2 pint)
5 oz (150 g) flour
4 eggs

Bring the water to the boil in a small saucepan, add the butter. Put the flour in the bowl, process for 2 or 3 seconds, and with the motor running pour the hot, boiling water and butter through the feed-tube. It should form an instant paste, return it to the saucepan and stirring cook gently for 3 or 4 minutes. Put the mixture back into the bowl and, with the motor running, add the eggs one at a time through the feed-tube. The pastry should now be pale gold and like very, very sticky thick cream. Either take it up in tablespoons and place on a greased baking tray in dollops, in long sausage-shapes for eclairs or use an icing bag with a 1/2 in. nozzle and pipe the shapes you want directly onto the tray. Either way, put the tray into a mark 7, 425°F, 225°C oven and leave to cook for 25 minutes. They will rise so make sure that you have left enough space for them. When they're cooked and golden brown, take them out of the oven and prick a hole with a skewer or a knife at the top of each to let the steam escape and keep the shell crisp and firm.

eclairs

4 oz (100 g) bitter chocolate
1 oz (25 g) butter
1 fl oz water
1 tablespoon icing sugar
1 recipe choux pastry

The long thin sausage-shapes are perfect for making eclairs. When they have cooled a little split them along one side carefully with a knife. Melt together the chocolate, butter, water and icing sugar and allow it cool slightly, before pouring carefully in a thin ribbon down each eclair, spread it with a pallet knife which has been dipped in hot water so that it keeps the chocolate melted and smooth. If you have any chocolate left over, you can go back and put a second coating on, which is extremely greedy, but very delicious. When the chocolate is cool (do not put it in the fridge, let it cool in the kitchen), fill the centre of the eclairs either with crème pâtissière or whipped cream. Crème pâtissèrie will keep a little longer, but the cream is perhaps a little more sumptuous.

Eclairs filled with whipped cream and double dipped in chocolate

profiteroles

Perhaps one of the most widely enjoyed restaurant sweets in the world. Profiteroles are really mini eclairs filled with whipped cream and with the chocolate coating still hot when they're eaten. They're a little trouble to prepare as they have to be done at the last minute, but well worth it for a grand case of showing off at a special dinner party.

1 recipe choux pastry
5 oz (150 g) double cream, whipped with
2 oz (50 g) castor sugar
4 oz (100 g) bitter chocolate
2 oz (50 g) butter
top of the milk from a gold (Jersey) pinta
grated rind of an orange

Make the choux pastry and bake it on a greased baking tray as 24 tiny walnut size balls. When these are cooked pierce the top of them with a skewer to let the steam out. When they're cool split each in half, and fill with the whipped cream. A dessertspoonful will go into each. Stack them if you can using a little of the cream as a kind of mortar into a shallow pyramid, and put aside. When you're ready to serve, melt the chocolate in the butter, add all the other ingredients and stir until thoroughly amalgamated and smooth before quickly pouring it over the profiteroles. It is quite possibly one of the most fattening dishes in the entire world, and for its devotees, amongst whom I am one, well worth it.

A hamper full of breads

bread is beautiful

Making bread with a processor is a real revelation. It's an amazing machine for a lot of cooking, but for bread making it is *revolutionary*. It also produces bread that is actually better than any I have ever managed by hand, especially in terms of texture. This is because, you get a fast thorough kneading of the dough that would require fifteen to twenty minutes hard, wrist aching work by hand. As any baker's manual will tell you it's the kneading that makes the difference between average and really good bread. All these recipes will produce bread with a fine even textured crumb, and a well matured flavour. The kind of flavour that makes it difficult to go back to shop bought bread at any time.

A couple of points about working bread at home. Buy the right kinds of flours. If you are buying wholemeal make sure it's a wholemeal intended for bread and includes what is known as durum wheat, which helps to produce a firm, well risen loaf. If you're buying white flour try and buy unbleached bread flour, it produces a perfectly white loaf, with a much richer flavour than the more ordinary commercial bleached varieties. If you can find it, try the wheatmeal loaf, made with flour that's had only 15% of the bran extracted. It produces what I think is probably the most delicious bread of all, well risen and as light as white bread, yet with a nuttiness and flavour of a good wholemeal. Most of the breads here are yeast risen and made with instant dried yeast which is just as good and produces bread that is usually indistinguishable from that made with the more normal dried yeast or with fresh yeast. The yeast risen breads all have instructions for using 12 oz (350 g) flour and 1/2 a packet (1 teaspoon) of instant yeast. If you have one of the bigger processors, with a large capacity, you can double this and use 1½ lb (700 g) flour and a whole packet of instant yeast. You can, if you prefer, use dried rather than instant yeast and you will need 1½ teaspoons for every 12 oz (350 g) of flour. Dried yeast, of course, will need sprinkling over warm water and sugar or treacle and then being left to foam up before use.

One of the lovely things about making bread with a processor is that although it only takes you a couple of minutes work, the lovely traditional processes that produce rich flavoured bread, will look after themselves while you do something else. If you havn't got the couple of hours to let the bread rise properly you can always try the soda breads that I have suggested, equally delicious in their own right. Do give a try to one of the more unusual recipes, like the herb and onion bread which is splendid eaten with farmhouse cheese, or as an accompaniment to a bowl of one of the richer soups, pages 18-27.

wheatmeal bread

This is made from flour which has had part of the bran extracted, but has enough left in it to give it both body and flavour, while allowing it to rise and produce the kind of texture that we are used to with white bread. It's sold marked 81% or 85% flour and most good supermarkets and almost all health food type stores stock it these days. I think it's the perfect compromise between wholemeal goodness and white bread luxury.

Double-bladed knife
12 oz (350 g) 81% or 85% flour
8 fl oz (250 ml) warm water
1/2 packet (1 teaspoon) instant dried yeast
1 teaspoon salt
1 tablespoon oil
1 tablespoon golden syrup

Put the flour, yeast and salt into the bowl and add the golden syrup and the oil to the hot water. Process the flour and with the motor running add the golden syrup, oil and water mixture. Continue processing for about a minute then put the dough in a greased bowl, and cover with a sheet of cling-film. Leave it in a warm place for about an hour to an hour and a half when it should double in size. Knock it down, punching it until all the air comes out of it, put it back in the bowl, which doesn't need to have been washed, and process it for another 30 seconds. Take it out and shape it into a round about six inches across and domed in the middle. Cut a gash in it with a sharp knife, and put it back in the warm place to rise for about 35 to 40 minutes, when it should again almost double in bulk. Put it into a preheated oven, gas mark 5, 375°F, 190°C and turn the heat down to mark 4, 350°F, 180°C. It should take about 40 minutes to bake, giving off the most wheaty aroma towards the end, do not be tempted to under cook it because of the smell. Test it by lifting it up and tapping the bottom, which should sound hollow, a test for almost all bread. If it's ready take it out let it cool on a wire rack, if not give it another 5 or 10 minutes in the oven. This bread keeps marvellously and is delicious toasted.

white bread

This is a recipe for white bread and there is really no better description except that compared to what you may have bought in the baker's, this is going to be a surprise. It will have a pale cream coloured crumb and a rich flavour, that makes anything more than salty butter and the privacy of your own kitchen seem unnecessary. It improves with a day's keeping before eating it, so if you can stand it, don't let the marvellous baking smell make you tear it to pieces just after it comes out of the oven.

Double-bladed knife
12 oz (350 g) unbleached white bread flour
7 fl oz (250 ml) warm water
1/2 packet (1 teaspoon) instant dried yeast
1 teaspoon salt
1 tablespoon softened butter

Put the flour, yeast, butter and salt into the bowl. Switch on and process for about 5 seconds. With the motor running pour the water in through the feed-tube. The dough will form a ball around the knife. Leave the machine on to thoroughly knead it for about a minute. Grease a bowl, take out the ball of dough, which should stick together, add any little bits that may have fallen off it, roll it in the oiled bowl, cover it with a piece of film and put it in a warm draught-free place, an airing cupboard is ideal, leave it to rise for about an hour. When it has doubled in size it's ready for the next process. Put it back in the bowl which need not have been washed in the meanwhile, knock it flat, so all the air comes out of it, it's really rather like punching a pillow, put the cover on and process again for another 30 to 45 seconds. Take out and put in a ready greased 1 lb (450 g) loaf tin (or a non-stick one, which I really think is even better). Put it back in the warm place, with a plastic cover over it if you like, and leave it until it's risen and has filled the tin. Preheat the oven to mark 7, 425°F, 220°C. As soon as the bread has reached the top of the tin, place it in the oven and turn the heat down to mark 6, 400°F, 200°C. It should be ready in approximately 35 to 40 minutes, but you do need to test, because some ovens and some flours differ. The way to do it is to turn the loaf on its side and so that it slides out of the tin, tap it on the bottom, if its sounds hollow, it's cooked, if not leave it out of its tin, it doesn't need it to shape it anymore. Let it bake for another 10 minutes or so. When it is cooked take it out and cool it on a wire rack or across the tin so the air can circulate right the way round it.

Brown soda bread *(see page 112)* **is especially good eaten warm and thickly spread with butter**

Putting the flour into the bowl

Measuring out the yeast

wholemeal bread

Traditionally wholemeal breads always seem difficult to make, and indeed only too often come out like leaden cake rather than proper bread. There is no way a real wholemeal is ever going to be as light or as delicately textured as white bread because the very ingredients that make it *whole*meal give it a bite and a solidity that the white flour has had removed. With a processor it is possible to have wholemeal bread with a lovely firm delicate texture, the kind that really does need to be eaten in large chunks with home-made chutneys and farmhouse cheeses. Don't be tempted to process this dough too long, wholemeal doesn't require anything like the kneading or processing that more refined flours need, and it's meant to be a wetter dough in the first place as well.

Double-bladed knife
12 oz (350 g) wholemeal flour (make sure it's bread flour)
1 tablespoon black treacle
½ packet (1 teaspoon) instant dried yeast
8 fl oz (250 ml) warm water
1 tablespoon oil
1 teaspoon salt

Put the flour, yeast and salt into the bowl, and process for about 5 seconds. Add the warm water to which you have added the black treacle and the oil and process for another 30 seconds by which time the mixture should look somewhat like a large mud pie, perhaps with a slightly thicker texture. If it's thoroughly blended don't process again, but take it out and place it in a large greased loaf tin or a non-stick one if you've got it. Put it in a warm place preferably covered with a greased plastic bag and leave it to rise for about 45 minutes to 1¼ hours. It should be just coming up to the top of the tin. Put it in a hot oven gas mark 7, 425°F, 220°C and bake it for 15 minutes, turn the heat down to gas mark 5, 375°F, 190°C, for another 30 minutes by which time the loaf should be cooked. Test it by tipping it out of the tin and tapping it on the bottom, once again it should sound hollow, if it doesn't leave it out of the tin, letting it bake for another 5 or 10 minutes until thoroughly cooked. It's best kept for a couple of days after being cooled on a wire rack or across the tin, but it can be eaten within four hours of it being baked.

Adding the treacle to the water and oil

Processed and kneaded dough

Putting the shaped loaf into the tin

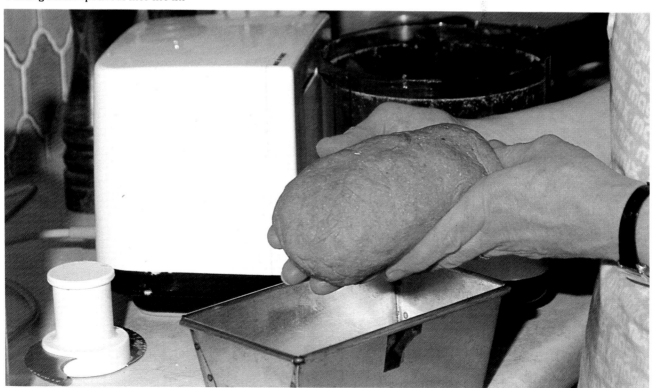

soda breads

These breads really come from the late nineteenth century, when artifical yeast as baking powder used to be known as then, suddenly became universally available. Ireland was the great place for Soda breads and indeed it still is. They don't call bread 'loaves' over there though, they call then cakes and they bake them fresh every day. None the worse for that either, for one of the great virtues of soda bread, is that you can have it on the table in less than an hour, after deciding that you wanted some in the first place. It's bread to be made in the shape of giant rolls. It doesn't work too well in bread tins and one of the attractions is the lovely crust it produces.

white soda bread

This perhaps is the explanation of why the Irish call soda breads cakes. It has a rather cakey texture, although not at all sweet, and is really nicest eaten straight out of the oven at tea time, with a sort of high tea fry up or lots of home-made preserves and honey. Traditionally it was made with buttermilk, the slightly soured cultured produce of the dairies that Ireland is so famous for. I find it works perfectly well with a mixture of milk and water and a tablespoon of yoghurt if you happen to have it to spare.

Double-bladed knife
1 lb (450 g) white flour (does not have to be special bread
    flour for this)
2 teaspoons baking powder
1 teaspoon bicarbonate of soda
1/2 pint (300 ml) mixed milk and water
1 tablespoon yoghurt
1/2 teaspoon salt

Put the flour and the salt and the baking powder in the bowl and process for 10 seconds, until thoroughly mixed. Add the water, milk and yoghurt, and process for 15 to 20 seconds, until the mixture forms a ball around the knife blade. Remove it, pat it firmly to make sure all the air is excluded, and shape it into one or two large rolls on a greased baking sheet. Cut a large cross on the top with a sharp knife and put into a preheated oven, mark 6, 400°F, 200°C without any time to allow it to rise. All the rising will take place in the oven. Bake it for 30 to 35 minutes, 20 to 25 if you are baking smaller cakes. Turn the oven down to gas mark 4, 350°F, 180°C and bake it for another 10 minutes. Make sure the cross doesn't burn, take it out and eat it while it's still warm. If you can't it can always be heated up for 5 or 10 minutes in the oven again.

brown soda bread

Very similar in method to the White Soda Bread. This produces a very different textured loaf. It's traditionally made in Ireland, with the very soft, coarsely ground wholemeal flour that they get there. Ordinary wholemeal is fine for us on this side of the water and an addition is a dessertspoon of soft brown sugar, which gives the bread a little sweetness. Don't be tempted to use Demerara, or any other kind of sugar, except genuine soft brown, otherwise the flavour will be lost and you'll just get a slightly sweeter loaf. I'm particularly fond of this bread at dinner parties where it can be produced almost straight from the oven, and sliced at the table, especially if the rest of the menu has got a rustic quality to it. It always produces 'Ooos' and 'Aaahs' and the only problem is you tend never to have any left, but then you can always make some the next morning so it's not too much of a hardship really.

Double-bladed knife
1 lb (450 g) wholemeal flour (coarser the better)
1/2 pint (300 ml) mixed milk and water
1 tablespoon plain yoghurt
1 dessertspoon soft brown sugar
1/2 teaspoon salt
2 teaspoons baking powder
1 teaspoon bicarbonate of soda

Put all the dry ingredients into the bowl and process for 10 seconds. Add the milk and water mixture in which you have dissolved the sugar. Process for another 10 seconds, scrape the sides down and process again for 5 seconds until thoroughly blended. Take out the dough, if it's not quite firm enough to handle properly, add a tablespoonful or two more of flour to the mixture with the motor running. It's often difficult to determine how much liquid different wholemeals will absorb in advance. When it's at the correct texture, shape it into two loaves, on a greased baking tray, and if you've got them, cover them with either large basins or cake tins inverted over the top of them. Put them straight into a preheated oven, mark 7, 425°F, 220°C and bake them for 30 minutes. Remove the tins or basins which will have helped the bread to rise quite spectacularly. Leave them to bake for another 10 minutes to set the crust and take them out of the oven. Cool them on a wire tray for about 10 or 15 minutes. You can eat them as soon as they are cool enough to cut, and if you want to reheat them in the oven the next day they still produce that lovely nutty flavour, that's so characteristic of this bread.

scones

In the West Country, these are normally eaten, stuffed with whipped cream and strawberry jam. They are also known in America as 'biscuits', and are eaten traditionally at breakfast time.

I have given a basic recipe here which you can add a variety of flavours and fillings some of which I suggest at the end.

Double-bladed knife
8 oz (225 g) plain white flour
2 oz (50 g) butter
1 tablespoon baking powder
pinch of salt
1 teaspoon castor sugar
1/4 pint (5 fl oz) milk

Put all the dry ingredients into the bowl and process for 5 seconds, add the butter and process again for 5 seconds. Pour in the milk, with the motor running, until the mixture forms a ball. If it forms a ball without using all the milk, stop then, if it needs a little more milk, add it, but very gently. Take it out and roll by hand, on a slightly floured board, into a cylinder about an inch and a half across. With a sharp knife cut the cylinder into inch thick rounds and place these on a greased baking tray, and pop them into a preheated oven mark 7, 425°F, 220°C. They should be ready in about 15 minutes, but if they are showing signs of browning before cooking fully inside, turn the oven down after 5 minutes to mark 5, 375°F, 190°C. They are really nicest eaten piping hot, straight out of the oven.

Variations:

1)   1/4 lb (100 g) of grated cheese added just before the milk, produces the most delicious cheese scones. Superb eaten with a little mango chutney mixed with the butter you spread on them.

2)   Fruit scones; an extra teaspoon of sugar an ounce each of currants, raisins, sultanas 4 oz (100 g) of mixed dried fruit. Add just after you've added the milk and knead in the processor for not more than 3 seconds. Makes a lovely fruit scone. I find these better not eaten hot but left to cool and mature for about four or five hours.

herb and onion bread

This is a very savoury loaf, delicious enough to eat on its own and especially good with a bowl of soup. You can vary the ingredients to suit what you happen to have growing in the garden, or on the pantry shelf, and you can use spring onions as opposed to the ordinary round ones I've suggested in the recipe. Indeed they give a lovely green fresh flavour to the whole loaf. Do experiment with this one, a clove of garlic, a little celery leaf, all produce breads of surprisingly delicate yet rich flavour.

Double-bladed knife
12 oz (350 g) white bread flour
1/2 packet (1 teaspoon) instant dried yeast
8 fl oz (250 ml) water
1 tablespoon oil
1 onion
up to 1/2 cup green herbs, mixture of parsley, thyme and
    oregano or marjoram – are my favourites
    If you are using dried herbs a generous teaspoon of
    each, with a double one of your favourite is about right
1 teaspoon salt

Peel and chop the onion in the bowl and fry it very gently in the oil until translucent, but not brown. Chop the herbs, if you are using fresh ones, in the processor for 10 seconds, scrape down the sides and chop again until finely processed for about another 10 seconds. Add the flour, yeast, the onion and a teaspoon of salt and process together for 5 seconds. With the motor running add the warm water. Knead for about a minute and a quarter, making sure half way through that all the ingredients are blended in thoroughly. Put to rise in a warm draught free place for about an hour, in a greased bowl. Process it again for just 30 seconds in the processor having knocked the air out of the dough first. Put it in a loaf tin, allow it to rise to double its volume. Bake it for 45 minutes in a preheated oven mark 6, 400°F, 200°C. Test it for being done, by tipping it out of the tin and tapping on the base when it should sound hollow. If it's not done give it another five or ten minutes. I have been known to put a layer of cheese slices along the top of this loaf about half way through cooking, after it's had a chance to rise and set properly in the oven, it makes Cheese, Herb and Onion loaf, but that's a personal self-indulgence and I suggest you only do it the second time you try.

Freshly cut slices of herb and onion bread

Streusel cake *(see page 118)*

crafty cakes

I must admit that until a processor came into my life I was no cake maker. All that creaming and beating and whipping seemed to me too much like hard work, and the results never light enough or delicate enough to be worth the trouble. With my new kitchen assistant, that just isn't true, and the cakes I produce I'm almost ashamed of, as it's quite possible to make one a day taking about 10 minutes to do it, and to continuously astound friends, relations and family with the results. The fact is that making cakes with a processor is probably quicker than reading about how to do it. All the recipes I've given here are my family favourites. I've not gone in for vast complicated gâteaux, although two or three of them are quite special enough to be served as puddings in their own right after a dinner party. The chocolate gâteau, for example, is really a kind of cold soufflé, and so rich that covered with whipped cream it makes a very grand pudding indeed. By and large these are family cakes, made with fairly inexpensive and easily available ingredients, but producing the kind of results that used to be seen only in the carefully staged colour photographs of the more expensive magazines.

streusel cake

This is a cake with a crumble topping. The crunchy topping and the soft rich cake make a lovely contrast. It's the sort of confection they serve with coffee in the famous cafés of Vienna and Salzburg, but it's quite good, I find, at coffee time in Walton-on-Thames or Selkirk. Either way, the secret, as usual is the processor which makes very light work of the two separate processes of rubbing in that have to be done to get the combination of textures.

Double-bladed knife
6 oz (175 g) plain flour
2 oz (50 g) cornflour
2 teapoons baking powder
4 oz (100 g) butter or soft margarine
4 oz (100 g) castor sugar
2 eggs
6 tablespoons milk

For the topping:
1½ oz (40 g) plain flour
2 oz (50 g) demerara sugar
1½ oz (40 g) butter
1 tablespoon cinnamon

Begin by making the topping. Placing the flour, sugar, cinnamon and butter in the bowl and process until it resembles very fine dry crumbs. Take it out and keep aside, then put all the cake ingredients – the flour, cornflour, baking powder, butter, sugar, egg and milk into the bowl, and process for 15 seconds, scrape down the sides, process again for another 10 seconds. Turn it into a buttered 7 in. (18 cm) cake tin or one of those Viennese style tins with a hole in the middle. Sprinkle the crumble mixture on the top and bake at mark 5, 375°F, 190°C for about an hour. When it's cooked turn it out carefully, being sure not to spill all the topping. You can eat this cake while it's still just a little warm, which when you consider the smells which it gives out when baking, is a great relief to the test of self-control.

marmalade cake

Another cake that's particularly useful for using up odds and ends. If you've got a couple of odd jars with bits of marmalade in the bottom and you can manage to get together three round tablespoons, you've got the basic ingredients for this cake. It's got a marvellous delicate flavour, and although it can be cooked in any container you like, it's best cooked in a loaf tin and sliced across into slices like bread. No butter needed with this one for it tastes quite rich enough without any help, thank you. As with most processor cakes, put all the ingredients in at the same time which keeps it light and avoids overbeating.

Double-bladed knife
8 oz (225 g) plain flour
1 teaspoon baking powder
4 oz (100 g) soft margarine or butter
3½ oz (90 g) sugar
2 eggs
3 large tablespoons orange marmalade (or a mixture of other marmalades and jams)
grated rind of a large orange
grated rind of a small lemon

Put all the ingredients into the bowl and process for 15-20 seconds. You may have bits of marmalade rind still left in the mixture, but don't let that worry you, as it will make delicious little nibbly bits. Tip the whole mixture into a large loaf tin, spread the top smooth, sprinkle with just a teaspoon or so of castor sugar, bake at mark 5, 375°F, 190°C for three quarters of an hour to an hour. You may need to bake it a little longer if the tin is particularly narrow and deep. Test it by running a skewer into it – it should come out absolutely clean. Cool on a wire rack.

Teatime with a chocolate gâteau, golden fruit cake, marmalade cake, chocolate biscuit cake and a victoria sponge with orange icing

three chocolate cakes

Chocolate cake always seems to be the favourite and these are very different, but each of them has a virtue of its own. One is from France, one from America and one from Belgium! I'll leave you to work out which is which, but do try all of them at some time or another.

oil chocolate cake

Made with a very unusual set of ingredients, this cake is incredibly rich and moist, especially if kept for about a week before eating. This does not happen in my house, but if you can manage two or three days, you will find that the cake, rather than drying out, absorbs moisture from the air and becomes yummy and delicious. It's the chocolate cake I suggest you ice if you're into iced cakes, and it's marvellous made in two sections in individual flan tins, and sandwiched together with butter icing flavoured with coffee. As for the ingredients you'll just have to trust me. They may sound unusual, but they work!

Double-bladed knife
6 oz (175 g) plain flour
3 heaped tablespoons cocoa
1 level teaspoon baking powder
1 level teaspoon bicarbonate of soda
5 oz castor sugar
1 level tablespoon black treacle
2 eggs
1/4 pint (5 fl oz or 150 ml) vegetable oil
1/4 pint (5 fl oz or 150 ml) milk

Mix all the dry ingredients, the flour, cocoa, baking powder, bicarb and castor sugar together. Process for 10 seconds until thoroughly blended, add the liquid ingredients and process again for 30 seconds, scraping the sides of the bowl until they are all thoroughly incorporated. Pour the mixture into two greased or non-stick 7 in. (18 cm) cake tins, bake in a medium oven mark 3, 325°F, 160°C, for 45 minutes. Cool and then sandwich with apricot jam, cream or butter icing as you choose.

chocolate biscuit cake

A no-cook cake made very easily, and with children the favourite one of all. I know few adults who've turned it down either! The combination of fresh orange zest with the richness of the chocolate is a classically successful combination, and as you can make it with the broken ends of biscuits left in the larder or the biscuit barrel, it can be a very economical proposition indeed.

Double-bladed knife
4 oz (100 g) margarine
4 oz (100 g) drinking chocolate
1 tablespoon each golden syrup, sultanas and raisins
1/2 orange
1/2 lb (225 g) sweet biscuits (I find ginger nuts and water biscuits equally mixed the best)
2 oz (50 g) chopped nuts (optional)

Put the orange, cut into quarters, peel and all, into the bowl, process until finely chopped scraping down the sides if you need to. Add the biscuits which do not need to be in one piece, process until they are finely broken up like coarse breadcrumbs. Melt the margarine and syrup, in a small saucepan and beat until it's smooth. Beat in the chocolate powder off the heat, add the sultanas, raisins and the chopped nuts if you're using them. Switch the motor on and pour the chocolate mixture into the processor. Process it long enough to mix it all thoroughly (about 7 seconds). Scrape it out and press it out into an oiled or non-stick flan tin about 8 in. (20 cm) across. It'll form a one inch cake which needs to be chilled in the fridge for at least three hours before eating.

chocolate gâteau

This cake is really masquerading under a false title. It's not a cake at all but a cold chocolate soufflé. Light and rich with only just enough flour in it to help it set properly, like many chocolate cakes it's best eaten a couple of days after it's made. In this case make sure you wrap the cake when it's cool in a tea towel and put it in a tin to store. You must be careful when you're incorporating the egg whites into the mixture, because processors beat so fast, they they can knock the air back out of them. I myself incorporate half the egg white in the processor, and fold the rest in by hand before pouring the cake into the tin to be baked.

Double-bladed knife
4 oz (100 g) each self raising flour, butter, castor sugar, chocolate, and four standard eggs

Melt the butter in a saucepan adding the chocolate broken up into bits. Stir it thoroughly as it melts, and don't do it over too high a heat so that the mixture doesn't really boil. When it's smooth, process for 5 seconds, add the sugar, process again for 15 seconds or until it's thoroughly blended. With the motor running, add the flour tablespoon by tablespoon. Separate the eggs and add the yolks to the chocolate mixture processing briefly to mix. In a separate basin whip the egg whites until they are so stiff that they stand in peaks. Add half of this to the chocolate mixture and process very briefly. Pour the chocolate mixture into the egg white basin and using a metal spoon fold in until the mixture is completely smooth. Pour it into a 7 in. (18 cm) diameter, well-greased cake tin, making sure that the tin is at least an inch and a half higher than the mixture, as it will rise spectacularly. Bake it at mark 6, 400°F, 200°C for 30–35 minutes. The top should be dark brown but not burnt when it's ready. Test it with a skewer which you push into the centre of the cake and which should come out clean with no mixture sticking to it. When it's cooked, put it on a rack and then wrap it in a tea towel and store it in a tin. A couple of days will improve its texture marvellously. You can eat it with a thick layer of icing sugar on the top, slavvered in double cream, or just as it is for a delicious, slightly gooey chocolate cake.

victoria sponge

Until the little kitchen helper came into my life sponges were always a mystery to me and came out like crunchy pancakes. Now crafty sponges flavoured with orange, lemon or even chocolate are a matter quite literally of three minutes plus the time they take to cook. My reputation is transformed and my waistline is totally destroyed. However, if you have a family that's used to practising self-denial or you don't really mind what happens to your shape, try making one or two variations of these special tea time treats.

Double-bladed knife
6 oz (175 g) soft butter or soft margarine
6 oz (175 g) sugar
3 eggs
6 oz (175 g) self raising flour

This is the basic recipe with alternatives further down.
Put all the ingredients into the mixing bowl and process for 10-15 seconds, scrape down the sides and process for another 10 or 15. Don't process it too long or the cake will become overbeaten and dry. Grease two sponge tins (or use non-stick), spread the mixture into them using the spatula to make sure it's even across the top, and bake at mark 4, 350°F, 175°C oven for about 25 minutes. Don't keep opening and shutting the door but near the end of the cooking time you can test the sponge by pressing it in the centre; if your fingermark vanishes and the sponge rises up again, it's cooked. Turn them onto a wire rack, to let them cool. My favourite method from now on, is to use one of those extremely expensive, delicious strawberry jams and spread it thickly in the middle before dusting the top with icing sugar, but you can follow your own inclinations. I'm afraid that's all there is to it. It really is as simple as it sounds and with a processor there's no way you can make it more difficult.

Variation:

Lemon Sponge

Grate the rind of half a lemon and cut the remaining half of lemon, peel and all into quarters. Before you put anything else into the bowl process the grated lemon rind and the half lemon for 20 seconds until you have a fine smooth mixture. Proceed as above adding the flour, fat, sugar and eggs and bake also as above. Lemon icing is nicest on top, with a thick layer of lemon marmalade in the middle. The jelly kind is fine, but if you can find some with peel it's even more delicious.

Chocolate Sponge

Dissolve three level tablespoons of cocoa in three tablespoons of hot water and add to the other ingredients before processing. When iced this makes a perfect cake for birthdays and celebrations.

Chocolate icing and decoration makes a very festive birthday cake

An all-in-one victoria sponge. Place the flour sugar and eggs in the bowl, process to mix, turn into a tin and bake until brown

banana teabun

Although you can eat this with butter, it's not really a bun at all, but a kind of rich fruity loaf shaped cake. It's also the perfect way for using up bananas that have gone over the hill a bit and are squashed, for even if the skins are completely black, they're still OK for this recipe.

Double-bladed knife
8 oz (225 g) self raising flour
1/2 teaspoon salt
4 oz (100 g) butter – softened
6 oz (175 g) castor sugar
6 oz (175 g) mixed dried fruit
2 eggs
1 lb (450 g) bananas

Put all the ingredients except the dried fruit into the bowl and process until they are all thoroughly amalgamated and the bananas chopped up fine: the odd chunk doesn't matter, but they shouldn't be in large pieces. Add the dried fruit and process for just 3 or 4 seconds to mix the fruit in, but not to chop it. Pour the mixture into a buttered or non-stick 2 lb (900 g) loaf tin, spread it out evenly and bake it at mark 4, 350°F, 175°C for an hour and a half. Let it cool before you tip it out of the tin, it'll keep for two or three days, with no harm at all, before you eat it.

Banana teabun is an especially moist and delicious cake

golden fruit cake

This recipe really is, I'm afraid, a cause for shame. It's like one of those cakes that people used to spend hours in the making but with a processor it can not be stretched out, once you've got the ingredients together, to more than a minute and a half, except of course for the baking time. The only thing to do is to pretend you don't have a processor, and spent two hours making the cake. No-one ever believes anything different anyway, because it just tastes too good. It's also the basis for even richer dark fruit cake for Christmas and birthday type celebrations, and I suggest at the end of the recipe a way of amending it to include that. The basic recipe though is pretty rich and delicious in its own right.

Double-bladed knife
6 oz (175 g) self raising flour
3 oz (75 g) soft brown sugar
3 oz (75 g) butter (softened) or soft margarine
1 1/2 tablespoons milk
2 medium eggs
1 teaspoon mixed spice
3 oz (75 g) *each* raisins, sultanas and mixed peel
1 oz (25 g) flaked almonds

Put the flour, eggs, butter, sugar and milk into the mixing bowl. Process for about 15 seconds, scrape down the sides of the bowl and process again for 10 seconds making sure that the whole mixture is thoroughly blended. Add the fruit, nuts and spice, process for just 5 seconds to blend them in, but not chopped up. Pour the whole mixture into an 8 in. (20 cm) greased cake tin (or a non-stick one), and cook in a slow oven mark 3, 325°F, 160°C for two hours before testing by running a skewer into the centre. It may need up to an extra half an hour's cooking. If the top starts to brown without the centre being finished, cover it with a little foil just to keep it from going too crisp. Cool it on a wire rack for at least two or three hours, and then either store it or ice it in any way you please.

celebration fruit cake

To the above recipe add, at the same time as the fruit, a tablespoonful of dark treacle, the grated juice and rind of a lemon and 2 oz (500 g) of glacé cherries. Bake as above. Some people find that washing the sugary bits off the outside of the cherries and then drying them helps to stop them sinking in the cake. Personally, I find that they sink or not as the wind takes them, and no amount of washing will stop it. Either way, they taste delicious and are worth it even in a delicate pink layer across the bottom of each slice.

proven puddings

These, as the song says, are some of my favourite things. I'm a great believer, like the French, in finishing a meal with a sweet taste in the mouth rather than the tang of cheese. I'm not a believer, however, in a great deal of hard work going in to making a pudding; by the time the rest of the meal is ready the cook needs a bit of a rest and relaxation too. This is a collection of puds, all of which can be made without a processor, but the processor will make it easier and quicker, so you won't finish up with a bunch of grapes to go with the cheese or a bought-in cake. These puds range from the grand, a very sophisticated Almond Mousse, through the rustic Clafoutis, to the extremely simple – the recipe for real custard which you really must try even if it's only to pour over an Apple Pie. With these creams, custards and fruit fools, presentation is crucially important and I'm very fond of using wine glasses; elegant and unusual ones, or if you haven't got glasses use white china or that very pale French porcelain which comes in tiny little soufflé dishes. Try and avoid fussy patterned crockery for these puddings, for the pale fruit colours look better against simple backgrounds.

Fruit fools *(see page 129)* **showing the contrasting colours of strawberry and blackcurrant**

Boodles fool

fruit fools

Why these puddings are called fools is something I've never actually been able to discover. What they are, is a very traditional mixture of fruit and cream or custard, blended together to make a particularly enticing and really rather rich dish. You don't need a lot of these. The flavour's very intense, and they're very filling.

boodles fool

Boodles was and still is one of the clubs for gentlemen in St James' in London, famous for its food, but no-one who's an outsider gets in to sample it. The odd recipe has escaped and this is one of them. It's a very simple one to make, dating back to the 17th Century, it's said. Serve it if you can in clear wine glasses with enough room for a good layer of the cake crumbs at the bottom before you pour on the orange cream.

Double-bladed knife
8 oz (225 g) sponge cake (dry is fine, but make sure it isn't
   too stale)
1/2 pint (300 ml) whipping cream
1/2 pint (300 ml) orange juice (carton is OK, tinned is not)
1/2 a whole orange

Put the sponge cake into the mixing bowl, and process to fine breadcrumbs. Tip out and mix with half the orange juice. Whip the cream, adding the remaining orange juice as you go, until the cream is beaten thick and all the juice is incorporated. Put the half orange into the bowl and process until it's finely puréed, and beat that into the cream as well. Put a portion of the crumbs into the bottom of each glass and pour over some of the cream. You can use a slice of orange from the other half to decorate each top. It's much the best if it's left to set in the refrigerator for about half an hour before it's served.

gooseberry fool

This is perhaps the most traditional of all English puddings. Apple tart and jam roly-poly not withstanding. It's very simple and very cheap, and ideally is made with custard (see page 130) as it used to be in the Middle Ages rather than with cream. Cream is fine though, but it produces a rather more delicate and sharp pudding. This is particularly nice served with very thin, crisp ginger biscuits.

Double-bladed knife
1 lb (450 g) fresh gooseberries (a tin will do, but it really isn't   the same)
6 oz (175 g) sugar
1/2 pint (300 ml) whipping cream or
   1/2 pint (300 ml) custard (it must be real)

Top and tail the gooseberries and wash them, putting them without any extra water into a pan. Add the sugar and simmer gently, the juice running out of the gooseberries will provide all the liquid you need. When they're cooked and squashy – about 15 minutes, pour the whole lot into the food processor. Switch on and process for 10 seconds, scrape down the sides and process again. The fruit should be thoroughly puréed although it may have a little texture left in it at the end if you like. If you're using cream, whip it until it's thick but not stiff and pour it into the bowl, switch on and process for 5 seconds. If you're using custard, let it get cold before adding it and process again in the bowl. This time you may need to process for a little longer, about 10 seconds is right. Pour the gooseberry fool either into china soufflé dishes or if you prefer, into wine glasses. Let it set in the fridge for at least an hour. It's a sharp, clean tasting dish, this, so reminiscent of spring-time in Britain.

You can substitute a whole range of fruit for the gooseberries; strawberries, blackcurrants and apricots are my favourites. The process is exactly the same, but you may want a little less sugar with fruit sweeter than gooseberries.

real custard

Believe it or not, custard didn't always come out of packets, and wasn't always that bright comic-strip yellow. Real custard is amazingly simple to make, extremely delicious to eat and funnily enough, it doesn't take much longer than the packet stuff. You can use it for many different purposes, eat it on its own, as a basis for the fruit fools which follow, replacing double cream, (a much cheaper way of making a fool and even less foolish!) or you can use it in the traditional way over a variety of tarts, pies or puddings.

Double-bladed knife
½ pint (300 ml) milk
1 tablespoon cornflour
1 egg
1 egg yolk
2 tablespoons castor sugar
1 teaspoon vanilla essence

Put the egg, egg yolk and vanilla essence into the bowl, switch on, and with the motor running add the cornflour and then the sugar. Bring the milk to the boil and just as it comes up, pour it in through the feed-tube, again with the motor running. Switch off after 3 or 4 seconds, when the mixture is thoroughly blended. Put it back into the saucepan and over a very low heat (you can use a double boiler for this) heat it gently. It'll thicken in about one minute and be cooked in about two. It can be eaten hot or cold, and is equally delicious either way.

clafoutis

A fantastic thick, crunchy pancake made traditionally in South Western France, with the bitter cherries that grow there and which have a short but splendid season. Unfortunately, we very rarely get those cherries over here, but this dish can be made with the black cherries that we do get or with apples mixed with cinnamon. It's particularly nice as a culmination to a family lunch or a big dinner party among friends when the food's had a strong rustic quality. It's not delicate, and it's pretty filling, so make sure the people who are going to eat it are hungry. It's also not a dish to keep waiting once it's cooked, as it is really at its best when it comes piping hot out of the oven.

The secret of a good clafoutis is the beating of the sugar and flour into the batter mixture so that it's really totally incorporated. A process which can take time, except for your friendly processor and the crafty clafoutis method.

Double-bladed knife
5 eggs
5 oz (150 g) *each* icing sugar and plain flour
1 lb (450 g) cherries (ideally stoned) or
1 lb (450 g) cooking apples, cored and peeled with
2 oz (50 g) sugar with a teaspoon cinnamon mixed with it
1 tablespoon oil

Break the eggs into the bowl, turn on and with the motor running add the icing sugar and flour tablespoon by tablespoon, one of each alternatively, through the feed-tube. The end should be a smooth batter. As soon as all the flour and sugar are added, add one tablespoon of oil and switch off. Butter a large baking dish or one of those crinkly-sided white china pie dishes. Pour in the batter mixture and sprinkle over it the cherries or the chopped up apple, cinnamon and sugar mixture. If you're using just the cherries, a little castor sugar sprinkled over the top will provide a nice caramelised grainy coating. Bake it in a mark 4, 350°F, 175°C oven for approximately an hour. It should be risen and golden to the touch, but the fruit should be buried in the crispy thick pancake.

A clafoutis makes an unusual hot pudding for a cold day

chocolate mousse

One of the dishes that has become debased in the course of time because everybody serves it and every restaurant has one, but very few people have ever tasted a perfectly made chocolate mousse. One of the reasons for this is, that in order to make one, an enormous amount of hard beating by hand has to take place, or at least it used to have to until processors pitched up in the kitchen. Do not skimp on the butter. It makes a great difference to the way this version of chocolate mousse tastes.

Double-bladed knife
7 oz (200 g) bitter chocolate (Bourneville's OK, Suchard or
    Terry's bitter chocolate is even better, there's less sugar
    in it)
3 oz (75 g) unsalted butter
6 eggs separated
juice and grated rind of an orange

Put the juice of the orange into a small heavy saucepan. Break the chocolate up into small squares, and add it to the juice and melt over a very low heat stirring all the time. When the chocolate has completely melted, add the butter and stir it in. When both are properly melted, pour the mixture into the bowl, switch on and process three times, 10 seconds each, scraping down the sides in between. This beating is very important and must go on until the whole chocolate mixture is smooth and glistening in texture. With the motor running add the egg yolks one at a time through the feed-tube, and process for a further 10 seconds before pouring the mixture back into the saucepan and stirring it over the very lowest heat for just one minute. (Do not let it boil or the eggs will scramble.) Whip the egg whites in a separate basin until they are so stiff you can turn the basin upside down and then gently fold the chocolate mixture into the egg whites, turning it all until it's all firmly mixed together. Add the grated rind from the orange, and pour into one large or six individual bowls and chill in the fridge for at least three hours.

home-made ice cream

Ice cream made at home is one of cooking's great revelations. Home-made bread and home-made soup join it as being one of the set of three things that are always better made at home. Part of the reason for this, is the quality of ingredients that you use, and although it may sound extravagant at first, you will find that because of its smoothness and richness a portion of ice cream goes a very long way. I've given a basic vanilla ice cream recipe, and three flavour variations, which I'm sure will all become fast favourites with your family. Your guests will enjoy them too, if your family will let them get to any.

Double-bladed knife
3 eggs
4 oz (100 g) icing sugar
1 teaspoon vanilla essence
5 oz (150 g) whipping cream

Break the eggs into the bowl, (you can if you want an even richer ice cream use up to 6 egg yolks replacing each egg with 2 yolks) add the vanilla essence, turn the motor on and feed the icing sugar in, tablespoon by tablespoon. Process until the mixture is a pale creamy yellow and very much thickened. Switch off and in a separate bowl whip the cream until it is thick but not stiff. Add the egg and sugar mixture to the cream and stir until thoroughly amalgamated. Pour it into a deep plastic bowl or container and put it into your freezer, if you've got one, or the freezing part of your fridge with the fridge turned up to maximum. It needs to freeze for at least 4 hours and afterwards will benefit from half an hour in the ordinary part of the fridge just before serving. If it sounds almost too simple, I'm afraid the only answer is that it is.

Additions and variations

You can add to this ice cream in a number of different ways. My favourites are fruit purées and the crunchy almond brittle known as praline. I'm going to give the recipe for strawberry ice cream but you can substitute peaches, apricots, raspberries or blackcurrants on condition that the purée you add is thick and creamy like pouring double cream. To achieve this, you may need to thicken one or two of the more watery fruits with a teaspoon of cornflour when you're cooking it. For one recipe of ice cream as above take:
1/2 lb (225 g) strawberries (which do not need to be in the prime of life), hull them, wash them and cook them with a tablespoon of sugar for about 3 or 4 minutes until the juice is just starting to run, process them to a purée and add them to the mixture of eggs and sugar before you mix it all

into the cream. After that, proceed exactly the same way chilling the mixture as before.

A sneaky ice cream flavouring which I'm very fond of, and one which is particularly nice in the winter when fresh fruit is not readily available is Marmalade. Very simply take some marmalade, about 4 tablespoons is right for one recipe of the ice cream mixture, ideally it should be one with a reasonable amount of peel in it, add it to the egg and sugar mixture and process for another few seconds until the marmalade is incorporated and the peel is cut into smaller size chunks, then proceed as above by adding it to the cream and then freezing.

praline

Very high-grade ice cream, this, the kind served in very delicate, very expensive cups in expensive restaurants. Put a knob of butter into a thick saucepan, preferably non-stick, and add 4 oz (100 g) of whole, unblanched almonds, toss them until they are coated with the butter and browned even more on the outside. Add 4 tablespoons of sugar and stir this into the almonds until it is thoroughly melted and the whole lot is beginning to pop. Be careful at this stage because if it pops onto you it can burn quite nastily. As soon as the sugar has caramelised and is starting to turn golden brown and toffee coloured, switch the heat off and leave the pan on one side. After 2 or 3 minutes immerse just the base of it in cold water. This will have the effect of contracting the pan suddenly and shaking the praline loose (that's why a non-stick pan is particularly advantageous at this stage). Tip it out onto a sheet of greaseproof paper and let it cool completely. When the praline's cool, break it into 1 in. chunks and process until it's really quite a fine powder. It'll make a noise doing this, but don't let it worry you, the machine can handle it quite easily. To make ice cream add the powder to the cream, not the egg mixture, before you fold it all in together. When you freeze it you can decorate it if you like with one or two of the larger chunks of praline that you may have kept aside.

shake it honey

Just to finish, a few milk shakes, both conventional and unconventional, to provide special treats for you and your family. While it's really not a standard blender the processors work perfectly well in this particular rôle and can manage to handle materials that an ordinary blender would blanch at. I've given a few recipes for children's-type milk shakes here, chocolate and strawberry, and one banana, lemon and honey flavoured one which I think they will really enjoy. There are also one or two grown-up milk shakes as well as the famous breakfast-in-a-glass recipe, that swept America recently and has been craftily adapted for our own use over here.

Avocado and pineapple shake *(see page 136)*

avocado and pineapple

A milk shake with a slightly sophisticated 'grown up' flavour. I'm sure the kids would like it, but in my house they don't get the chance. It can be served as a first course at a summer dinner party on a warm outdoor evening, but it's also nice as a milk shake in its own right.

Double-bladed knife
1 very ripe avocado
1 small tin pineapple chunks
5 oz (150 g) carton yoghurt
½ pint (300 ml) ice cold milk
sprigs of mint
pinch salt

Cut the avocado in half, remove the stone, and spoon the flesh into the bowl. Add the pineapple and the syrup from the tin, a pinch of salt (trust me) and the yoghurt and process for 15 seconds. Scrape down the sides and process again until smooth. Add the milk and process until the whole mixture is frothy. You can add a few of the mint leaves at this stage and process again for 2 seconds to mix them in, or you can leave them as sprigs to decorate the milk shake when you pour it into tall glasses. Chill it in the fridge for 30 minutes before serving it.

strawberry milk shake

Another standard favourite, but with the added bonus of fresh strawberries incorporated in it. You can use the strawberries raw or cooked as you please. I find that adults prefer the rather sharper taste of the raw strawberries, and kids the cooked version. Either way, the ingredients are the same.

Double-bladed knife
8 oz (225 g) strawberries hulled and washed
2 tablespoons castor sugar
4 oz (100 g) vanilla ice cream – not strawberry
    (dairy grade is best)
8 oz (225 g) cold milk

Save two or three of the prettier strawberries for decoration and if you want the children's version cook the strawberries and sugar together for two or three minutes until the juice is running. If you want the strawberries raw, put the strawberries and sugar straight into the bowl. Either way, purée the fruit and sugar mixture, add the ice cream and the cold milk all at once and process again until smooth. Decorate with the whole fresh strawberries, and chill in the fridge for 10 minutes or so before consuming. It's sometimes so thick this when you've finished that you have to eat it with a spoon. I find this no hardship.

chocolate milk shake

Straight out of the Macdonalds stable but much cheaper to make at home than to buy. You may need one of those enormously thick straws to drink it with, an ordinary straw just hasn't got a chance with the thickness of this particular shake.

Double-bladed knife
8 oz (225 g) chocolate ice cream
1/2 pint (300 ml) ice cold milk
bar chocolate flake

Put the milk into the bowl, add half the ice cream and switch on then add the rest of the ice cream through the feed-tube, spoonful by spoonful, until the shake is thoroughly blended. Don't process it for more than 25 seconds otherwise it may start to warm up a bit. Crumble the flake in your hand and add it through the feed-tube to the shake, saving enough to decorate the top. Pour it into tall glasses and sprinkle over the remaining flake bits. Put in the thick straws and duck, as the kids come rushing past you.

banana, lemon and honey

A simple, very nutritious shake, this one, which adults and children both seem to like. You can use old and fairly tired bananas for this recipe on condition that they're properly ripe.
Double-bladed knife
4 bananas
juice of a lemon
2 tablespoons runny honey
5 oz (150 g) yoghurt
5 fl oz (150 ml) milk

Peel the bananas and cut them into 1 in. slices, put them in the processor with the lemon juice and the honey. Start the motor and with it running add the yoghurt, then fill the yoghurt pot again with milk and add that. You'll get a golden coloured, very thick shake. If you like your shakes a little thinner add an extra measure of milk. Chill and serve in tall glasses with perhaps a banana slice or two on the top.

breakfast in a glass

An American habit, and not as nauseating as it sounds is a drinking breakfast. Too many people skip breakfast these days, because of pressure, time and also frankly lack of desire to eat a whole lot of greasy food early in the morning. This recipe gives you a light and delicious breakfast, which you really can drink from the glass. It's made in a trice and is full of good things as well as nice flavours. Particularly good, I find, as part of a weekend brunch when of course it isn't the whole of your breakfast but merely the start.

Double-bladed knife
1 whole orange
5 oz (150 g) plain yoghurt
2 teaspoons honey
1 egg
½ pint (300 ml) cold milk
2 dessertspoons of wheatgerm

Cut the orange into quarters, take out any pips, cut each quarter in half and put them into the bowl. Add the egg and yoghurt, and process until the orange is finely blended, (believe it or not, the peel won't taste bitter). With the motor running add the milk and then 2 tablespoons of runny honey. Blend again until smoothly mixed, pour into two glasses, and sprinkle the wheatgerm over the top. You can eat it with a spoon, or drink it. It's a slower process drinking than eating, but equally delicious either way. It can be made the night before and left in the fridge covered with a piece of cling-film, but add the wheatgerm at the last minute.

Adding honey to the breakfast in a glass mixture

Quite the best way to start the day

index

(figures in bold type indicate illustrations)

american apple pie, 100
apple and blue cheese dip, 16
apple pie, 100
artichokes provençale, jerusalem, 81
avocado dishes:
    and pineapple milk shake, **135**, 136
    blue cheese and apple dip, 16
    florida fruit plate, 50
    guacamole, 15

baker's cream, 101, 102
banana, lemon and honey milk shake, 137
banana teabun, 124, **124**
béarnaise sauce, 42
béchamel sauce, 40
beef dishes:
    cauliflower lasagne, 76
    chili con carne, 77
    hamburgers, 74
    italian meatballs, 77
    potted tongue, 35
    steak pizzaiolla, 71, **71**
    steak tartare, **72**, 74
    suprême of braised, 70
beetroot and yoghurt crudités, 51
blue cheese and apple dip, 16
boodles fool, **128**, 129
bread, **106**, 107–14
    herb and onion, 114, **115**
    soda, 112
    wheatmeal, 108
    white, 108
    wholemeal, 110
bread salad, 46, **47**
breakfast in a glass (milk shake), 137, **137**

cabbage salad, 50
cakes, 117–25
    banana teabun, 124, **124**
    celebration fruit, 125
    chocolate, 120–1, **121**, 123
    golden fruit, 125
    lemon sponge, 123
    marmalade, 118
    streusel, **116**, 118
    victoria sponge, 123
caroline's cheese pudding, 56, **56**, **57**
carrot soup, 21
carrots vichy, 81
carrots with meux mustard crudités, 52

cauliflower lasagne, 76
celebration fruit cake, 125
celery and walnut crudités, 52
cheese dishes:
    and apple dip, 16
    and date dip, 17
    cauliflower lasagne, 76
    potted, 35
    pudding, caroline's, 56, **56**, **57**
    quiche, 96
chicken dishes:
    chowder, chunky, 24
    liver pâtés, 32
    maryland, 66
    pie, 98, **98**, 99
    tandoori, 64, **65**
chili con carne, **15**, 77
chili ginger cabbage, 84
chinese cabbage salad, 50
chocolate:
    biscuit cake, 120
    gâteau, 121
    milk shake, 137
    mousse, 132
choux pastry, 104–5
    éclairs, 104
    profiteroles, 105
chowder, chunky chicken, 24
clafoutis, 130
coleslaw, 46
country pâté, 33
crab dip, 17
crème patissière, 101, 102
crisps, 13
crudités, 44–52, **45**, **53**
    beetroot and yoghurt, 51
    carrots and meux mustard, 52
    celery and walnut, 52
cucumber, minted, 51
custard, real, 130
cutlets milanese, 67

dips, 13–17, **12**, **14**, **15**
    blue cheese and apple, 16
    cheese and date, 17
    crab, 17
    egg and tomato, 16
    guacamole, 15, **15**
    sour cream and onion, 16
    yoghurt and mint, 14, **14**

dressings, 36, 38–9
    blue cheese, 38
    green mayonnaise, 39
    lemon, 38
    mayonnaise, **37**, 39, **39**
duck pâté en croûte, **28**, 30, **30**, **31**

éclairs, 104, **105**
egg dishes, 55–61
    and tomato dip, 16
    caroline's cheese pudding, 56
    mousse, 58
    sausage omelette, 61
    spanish omelette, **60**, 61, **61**
    smoked salmon scramble, 58, **59**
elana salad, 48, **48**, 49
english apple pie, 100

fancy fish soup, 22, **22**, **23**
fish dishes:
    crab dip, 17
    shrimps thermidor, 67
    smoked mackerel pâté, 33
    smoked salmon scramble, 58
    soup, fancy, 22, **22**, **23**
food processors, 10–11
    chipping disc, 11
    coleslaw or julienne cutter, 11
    double-bladed knife, 11
    grater, 11
    slicing disc, 11
fools, **see** puddings
french fruit tart, 102
french onion soup, 24, **25**
fruit dishes:
    clafoutis, 130
    fools, 129
    french fruit tart, 102

game pie, 97
gazpacho, 26, **27**
golden fruit cake, 125
goosebury fool, 129
gratin dauphinoise, 70
green mayonnaise, 39
guacamole, 15, **15**

hamburgers, 74
herb and onion bread, 114, **115**
hollandaise sauce, 42

ice cream, 132–3
italian meatballs, 77

jerusalem artichokes provençale, **79**, 81

kebabs, lamb, 76

lamb dishes:
   cutlets milanese, 67
   kebabs, 76
   saté, 68, **68**, **69**
   welsh honey roast, **62**, 64
lasagne, cauliflower, 76
leftovers, in spanish omelette, 61
lemon sponge, 123
lentil soup, 21
liver pâté, chicken, 32

mackerel pâté, smoked, 33
maltaise sauce, 42
marmalade cake, 118
mayonnaise, **37**, 39, **39**
   green, 39
meatballs, italian, 77
meux mustard and carrot salad, 52
milk shakes, 134–7, **137**
   avocado and pineapple, **135**, 136
   banana, lemon and honey, 137
   breakfast in a glass, 138, **138**
   chocolate, 137
   strawberry, 136
minced meat dishes, 73–7
   cauliflower lasagne, 76
   chili con carne, **15**, 77
   hamburgers, 74
   italian meatballs, 77
   lamb kebabs, 76
   steak tartare, **72**, 74
mint and yoghurt dip, 14
minted cucumber, 51
mornay sauce, 40
mousse:
   chocolate, 132
   egg, 58

oil chocolate cake, 120
omelettes:
   sausage, 61
   spanish, **60**, 61, **61**
onion:
   and sour cream dip, 16
   quiche, **91**, **94**, 95, **95**
   sauce (soubise), 40
   soup, french, 24, **25**
orange and tomato soup, 21

parsley sauce, 40
party food, 63–71
   chicken maryland, 66
   cutlets milanese, 67
   saté, 68, **68**, **69**
   shrimps thermidor, 67
   steak pizzaiola, 71, **71**
   suprême of braised beef, 70
   sweet corn fritters, 66
   tandoori chicken, 64, **65**
   welsh honey roast lamb, **62**, 64
pasta dishes:
   italian meatballs, 77
   lasagne, 76
pastry, 90–105
   choux, 90, 104–5
   french savoury (pâte brisée), 90,
      92, **92**, **93**
   shortcrust, 90, 97, 98, 100
   sweet (pâte sablée), 90, 101, 102
pâte brisée, 90, 92, **92**, **93**, 95, 96
   cheese quiche, 96
   onion quiche, **91**, **94**, 95, **95**
   quiche provençale, 96
pâte sablée, 90, 101, 102
   french fruit tart, 102
   strawberry tart, 102, **103**
pâtés, 29–33
   chicken liver, posh, 32
   chicken liver, rustic, 32
   country, 33
   duck, en croûte, **28**, 30, **30**, **31**
   smoked mackerel, 33
pommes dauphinoise, 85, **86**, **87**
potage bonne femme, 20
potato galette, 84, **85**
potted cheese, 35
potted meats, 29, **34**, 34–5
   tongue, 35
   turkey, 35
praline, 133
processors, food, 10–11
profiteroles, 105
puddings, 126–34
   boodles fool, **128**, 129
   clafoutis, 130
   custard, 130
   gooseberry fool, 129
   ice cream, 132–3
   milk shakes, 134–7, **137**
   praline, 133
punchep, 89
purées, 88–9
   punchep, 89
   spinach à la crème, 88, **89**
   sprout, 88

quiches, 95–6
   cheese, 96
   onion, **91**, **94**, 95, **95**
   provençale, 96

ratatouille, **79**, 80, 96

salads, 44–52, **45**
   beetroot and yoghurt, 51
   bread, 46, **47**
   carrots with meux mustard, 52
   celery and walnut, 52
   chinese cabage, 50
   coleslaw, 46
   elana, 48, **48**, **49**
   florida fruit plate, 50
   waldorf, 47, **47**
salmon scramble, smoked, 58, **59**
saté, 68, **68**, **69**
sauces, 36–43, **40**, **41**
   béarnaise, 42
   béchamel, 40
   hollandaise, 42
   maltaise, 42
   mornay, 40
   onion, 40
   parsley, 40
   soubise, 40
   tomato, 43, **43**
   white, 40
sausage omelette, 61
scones, 113
shortcrust pastry, 90, 97, 98, 100
   american apple pie, 100
   chicken pie, 98
   english apple pie, 100
   game pie, 97
shrimps thermidor, 67
smoked mackerel pâté, 33
smoked salmon scramble, 58, **59**
soubise sauce, 40
soups, 18–27
   carrot, 21
   chunky chicken chowder, 24
   fancy fish, 22
   french onion, 24, **25**
   gazpacho, 26, **27**
   lentil, 21
   potage bonne femme, 20
   spinach, 20
   tomato and orange, 21
   vichysoisse, 26
sour cream and onion dip, 16
spanish omelette, **60**, 61, **61**
spinach:
   à la crème, 88
   soup, 20

sprout purée, 88
sprouts polonaise, 78, **79**, 80
steak:
 pizzaiolla, 71, **71**
 tartare, **72**, 74
strawberry:
 milk shake, 136
 tart, 102
streusel cake, **116**, 118
suprême of braised beef, 70
sweet corn fritters, 66

tandoori chicken, 64, **65**
tomato:
 and egg dip, 16
 and orange soup, 21
 guacamole, 15
 sauce, 43, **43**

tongue, potted, 35
turkey, potted, 35

vegetables, 78–90
 carrots vichy, 81
 chili ginger cabbage, 84
 jerusalem artichokes
  provençale, **79**, 81
 mixed fried, 82, **82**, 83
 pommes dauphinoise, 85, **86**,
  87
 potato galette, 84, **85**
 purées:
  punchep, 89
  spinach à la crème, 88,
   89
  sprout, 88
 sprouts polonaise, 78, **79**, 80
 ratatouille, **79**, 80

vichysoisse soup, 26
victoria sponge, 123
waldorf salad, 47, **47**
walnut and celery salad, 52
welsh honey roast lamb, **62**, 64
white sauce, 40

yoghurt:
 and beetroot salad, 51
 and mint dip, 14
 and minted cucumber, 51
 in tandoori chicken, 64